Cou... ...ds of

WEST VIRGINIA

Drives, Day Trips, and Weekend Excursions

Lynn Seldon

COUNTRY ROADS PRESS

NTC/Contemporary Publishing Group

Library of Congress Cataloging-in-Publication Data

Seldon, W. Lynn, 1961–
    Country roads of West Virginia : drives, day trips, and weekend
excursions / Lynn Seldon.
        p.   cm. — (Country roads)
    Includes index.
    ISBN 1-56626-122-8
    1. West Virginia—Tours.   2. Automobile travel—West Virginia—
Guidebooks.   3. Rural roads—West Virginia—Guidebooks.   I. Title.
II. Series.
    F239.3.S45   1998
    917.5404'43—dc21   98-23335
                                                                  CIP
                                                                  r98

Cover illustration copyright © Todd L. W. Doney
Interior illustrations copyright © Barbara Kelley
Cover and interior design by Nick Panos

Published by Country Roads Press
A division of NTC/Contemporary Publishing Group, Inc.
4255 West Touhy Avenue, Lincolnwood (Chicago), Illinois 60646-1975 U.S.A.
Copyright © 1999 by Lynn Seldon
Printed in the United States of America
International Standard Book Number: 1-56626-122-8
98 99 00 01 02 03 ML 19 18 17 16 15 14 13 12 11 10 9 8 7 6 5 4 3 2 1

To the People of West Virginia

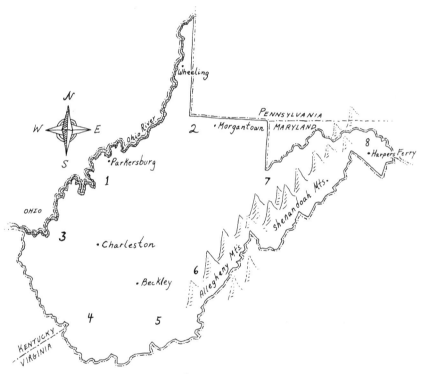

West Virginia Country Roads
(Figures correspond with chapter numbers.)

Contents

Introduction

Ask anyone who's been there about West Virginia. It just takes one visit to fall in love with this wild and wonderful state. I fell in love with West Virginia on my first visit and I've been back more than a hundred times. If I don't end up moving there, I'll get back there as often as possible.

My father's side of the family has West Virginia roots and I can feel it in my blood every time I cross the state border from my home in Virginia. The West Virginia mountains and the proud people get in your blood and it's a very warm feeling.

The number of West Virginia lovers is growing quickly as word spreads about what the state has to offer. Visitors are drawn to incredible natural beauty, a wealth of outdoor recreation opportunities, many historical attractions, an excellent state park system, friendly people, and a simpler and slower-paced way of life.

Coal may have once been king in the Mountaineer State, but tourists are now treated like royalty in West Virginia. Tourism is the second largest industry (behind chemicals) and the fastest-growing segment, as new and old visitors explore the state.

Convenient interstate routes in West Virginia make access easier than many drivers assume. The exploration possibilities are extensive, but all are within a one-day drive of half the population in the United States. The state's beauty is definitely worth the drive.

From friendly cities to rugged mountains, West Virginia is a welcome change. Each region offers its own outdoor and indoor pleasures, but the entire state definitely deserves the nickname, "Almost Heaven."

The Eastern Panhandle

Washington, D.C.–dwellers love the eastern panhandle of West Virginia. It's close to the urban hubbub, but it's another world for visitors.

The Harpers Ferry National Historic Park provides a perfect introduction to the historical richness of the state. Situated at the confluence of the Shenandoah and Potomac Rivers in the shadow of the Blue Ridge Mountains, Harpers Ferry became an important industrialized transportation hub and arms-producing town in the eighteenth and nineteenth centuries. The town came to national prominence in 1859 as the setting of abolitionist John Brown's attempt to liberate slaves through violence. Brown was captured and eventually hanged.

After the Civil War, many people left war-ravaged Harpers Ferry, which suffered additional damage from a series of devastating floods in the late 1800s. It fell into decay before a major restoration effort by the government.

Today, the Harpers Ferry National Historic Park is a national treasure. The restored historic buildings, exhibits, shops, and restaurants are among the most-visited sites in the nation. The park is perfect for an extensive walking tour. For hikers and cyclists, the Appalachian Trail and the C&O Canal are nearby.

The rest of the eastern panhandle offers more scenic and historic possibilities. Cacapon State Park features a great golf course designed by Robert Trent Jones and plenty of other outdoor activities. Many small towns and villages, such as Charles Town, Shepherdstown, and Keyser, offer quiet getaways.

For complete rejuvenation, head for Berkeley Springs. This historic spa town is a great weekend getaway. Relaxing spa treatments and much more are available at Berkeley Springs State Park, the Country Inn, and Coolfont Resort.

The Potomac Highlands

Heading into the heart of West Virginia means heading for the mountains. The Potomac highlands offer many year-round recreational opportunities.

Canaan Valley State Park is the region's outdoor mecca. The unique park and nearby outfitters offer downhill and cross-country skiing, golf, hiking, biking, and other warm-weather activities, many accommodation options, and lots of sheer beauty. Nearby, Blackwater Falls State Park has many park pleasures and beautiful falls plunging more than five stories.

Farther south, more mountain adventures await. The Dolly Sods Wilderness Area lies on a high plateau in the Monongahela National Forest, featuring a unique landscape and climate similar to a Canadian tundra. Nearby, Seneca Rocks towers more than 900 feet, offering internationally known rock climbing on Tuscarora sandstone dating to the Silurian Age.

The Snowshoe Mountain Resort area is fast becoming a four-season outdoor mecca, with great skiing, golf, and much more. At the base of the mountain, Elk River Touring Center offers great cross-country skiing in the winter and mountain-bike tours when the snow melts.

Drivers who want a short break from the road should try the Cass Scenic Railroad. This steam locomotive train carries passengers through the mountains to the summit of Bald Knob, the state's second highest peak.

Mountaineer Country

The football team from West Virginia University, the Mountaineers, has introduced the nation to Morgantown, but this area features much more than a great college town and atmosphere. Along with the cultural center of Morgantown, Mountaineer Country features many small towns and big outdoor adventures.

Morgantown is a modern college city steeped in history and surrounded by the mountains. Along with the university, downtown Morgantown features lots of historic sites and many arts and crafts shopping spots.

Many small surrounding towns make for an ideal driving tour of the countryside. Grafton was the site of the first Mother's Day observance in 1908 and now is home to the International Mother's Day Shrine. Clarksburg, Fairmont, and Mannington are other popular historic stops.

With so many mountains, visitors expect to find outdoor activities. Tygart Lake, the state's largest, is the base for many possibilities. Along with boating and lakeside pursuits, whitewater rafting is big business in the area. The Tygart and Cheat Rivers offer some of the most challenging white water in the East.

The Northern Panhandle

The northern panhandle of West Virginia is still a big part of the tourism picture. This historic crossroads region played host to many pioneers heading west. Today, locals play host to the tourists exploring this history.

Located along a beautiful riverfront, Wheeling was the hub of the state's western gateway. This lively city thrived during a time when Victorian architecture was popular. Many of the homes and businesses have been restored, making for one of America's great concentrations of Victorian-style architecture.

Wheeling is also known for Oglebay Park. This municipal park is much more than a typical city park. It's more like a resort, with three championship golf courses, a par-three course, swimming, hiking, boating, horseback riding, a zoo, and accommodations—all spread over more than 1,500 acres.

While Wheeling is definitely worth at least a weekend, the rest of the panhandle also deserves attention. Historic towns, including Wellsburg, Weirton, Newell, Moundsville, New Martinsville, and Sistersville, all draw today's tourists.

Mid-Ohio Valley

The frontier culture and pioneering spirit are also alive and well in the westernmost portion of the state. Many people were lured to the riches of the Ohio River and the surrounding valley. They still are today.

Parkersburg serves as an ideal base for modern-day explorers. This historic city has always been the area's civilized center. Highlights include the Oil & Gas Museum, the Tillinghast Cook House, the Little Kanawha Craft House, and the Blennerhassett Hotel.

Just outside the city sits a monument to the early boom days of Parkersburg. The Blennerhassett Island Historic State Park was once the huge estate of the region's wealthy early residents, Harman and Margaret Blennerhassett. Today, a sternwheel boat carries visitors to the reconstructed mansion and grounds.

The rest of the region's possibilities include historic Williamstown, the natural wonders of the Ohio River Border Islands National Wildlife Refuge, the bass fishing at St. Marys, and Ripley's huge Mountain State Art and Craft Fair on Independence Day weekend.

Mountain Lakes

The center of the state is all wet. The many lakes and related water sports are the centers of attention for this pretty region.

Summersville Lake, the state's largest, is a popular choice. Fishing, boating, waterskiing, and camping are all easy to coordinate. Scuba diving in the lake's clear water is also quite popular.

Summersville Dam, at 390 feet in height and 2,280 feet in length, is the second highest rock-fill dam in the United States. In the fall, water releases create one of the nation's great white-water rafting trips on the Gauley River.

Metro Valley

There's more to the Mountaineer State than the great outdoors. The state's capital, Charleston, and the inland port city of Huntington cast a cosmopolitan shine on the state.

Charleston has a friendly urban face. The gold-domed capitol complex overlooks the many restored buildings and the lazy Kanawha River. From Old Charleston Village to the East End historic district, this city still maintains West Virginia's country charm.

To the west, Huntington has grown into a well-planned industrial city. The city is known for its port operations, beautiful homes, thriving cultural environment, Marshall University, and the nearby historic community of Ceredo.

The rest of the region offers West Virginia's trademark mountainous beauty. This is coal country, with many of the nation's major coal fields and the historic coal town of Matewan.

New River and Greenbrier Valley

The New River and Greenbrier Valley region is a microcosm for the entire state, with outdoor splendor and lots of history. The modern interstate system now makes this region easier to explore.

Many modern-day explorers head right for the New River. Ironically one of the oldest rivers on the continent, the New River Gorge National River cuts a deep gorge through this part of the state. It's known for its scenic beauty, history, rock climbing, fishing, and world-famous white-water rafting. It's also known for the New River Gorge Bridge, the second highest bridge in the country and the longest steel-arch bridge in the world. Each year, the bridge is closed on the third Saturday of October for Bridge Day, when parachutists and bungee jumpers can enjoy high-flying fun.

More subdued diversions can be found throughout the region. Some options include the Beckley Exhibition Coal Mine, the Lewisburg historic districts, the Hinton historic district, and many state parks.

One of the state's most famous diversions is also in this neck of the woods. Located in historic White Sulphur Springs, the Greenbrier has been one of America's classic resorts since the early 1800s. The resort offers elegant accommodations, an old-world atmosphere, first-rate cuisine, and the Greenbrier Spa and Mineral Baths and Salon. It's a great way to end a visit to West Virginia.

Preparing this book renewed my immense love for everything West Virginia has to offer. My companion for every mile and word was my soulmate and wife, Cele. When I refer to "we" in the text, you can assume it is the two of us. We've driven more than 4,000 miles in search of perfect country road drives.

I've chosen a variety of routes to expose readers to the variety of experiences the state offers. Thus, you'll find a country road to pursue almost any special love you want.

However, please keep in mind that logistics and length kept some fine West Virginia destinations from being included. Many accommodations and sightseeing options I know and love simply couldn't be included because of the book format. But that means there are many places for you to discover on your own near many of my country road drives.

The interstate system allows you to get to country roads quickly. That means you'll have more time to pursue my recommendations and many of your own discoveries. Allow the time to linger by staying a night or more.

My research and travels for this book put me in contact with some great resources that can help other country road lovers. I highly recommend contacting tourism organizations for information and tips to make your own drives even more enjoyable.

Quite simply, West Virginia has one of the best tourism departments in the United States. Visitors should take full advantage of the vast amount of written material available for the state. For further information about visiting the state, contact the West Virginia Division of Tourism at 2101 Washington St. E., Charleston, WV 25305. Better yet, you can use the fantastic (800) CALL WVA calling service or the Internet site (http://www.state.wv.us) to meet most of your needs.

I highly recommend staying in the bed and breakfasts, small inns, and at other local accommodation options throughout the state. There are many excellent books about B&Bs, as well as several organizations.

This book could not have been written without the help of many special people. Everywhere we went in the state, we told people about the project and they did their best to make the book better for future visitors. The places of the state are quite special, but the people make them memorable. From natives who decide to stay to others who come for a visit and never leave, the state is full of special people doing special things for tourists.

Special thanks go to Cindy Harrington, travel media director with the state's tourism office, whose love of the state matches mine and who made my research trips productive and enjoyable. This book could not have been written without Cindy. Steve Shalutta and David Fatalleh, two of the state's fine photographers, helped me translate many of my wonderful West Virginia experiences onto film.

Dave Arnold, co-founder and co-owner of Class VI River Runners, gave me many ideas for the book. As is typical of many business owners in West Virginia, he is passionate about what the state has to offer and spreads the good word wherever he goes. When I think of my many wonderful trips to West Virginia, Dave always comes to mind. Rafting with Class VI in West Virginia is a first-class experience.

I would like to thank Ray Jones at Country Roads Press for allowing me to write this book and supporting the creative process. Many of my friends in Virginia and West Virginia have contributed some great ideas that made their way into the book. My parents and family contributed a love of our sister state and support of this travel-writing dream that I have somehow made a reality.

My wife, Cele, has been there for me, on the road and at the computer, for the entire project. In many ways, this book is our joint project and a gift of thanks to the state for having so many wonderful country roads to explore.

—WLS

1

Along the Ohio River

Getting there: From Charleston, take I-79 north and I-70 west to Ohio's Route 7 north for the start of the drive on Route 2 in Chester. To avoid backtracking, you could start the drive in Wheeling and skip the portion between Chester and Wheeling (saving several hours, but missing several interesting small towns). You can also start the drive at the other end in Huntington.

Highlights: Views along the Ohio River, Newell's Homer Laughlin China Company, Wellsburg, Bethany, Wheeling's Oglebay Resort, Moundsville, Sistersville, Parkersburg, Point Pleasant, Huntington. This drive is easily completed in two or three days, with overnight stays along the way (for example, in Parkersburg) or in Wheeling or Huntington at the start or end of the drive.

The northern panhandle is distinctly West Virginia, though it's greatly influenced by the Ohio River and the neighboring states of Ohio and Pennsylvania. A drive along the Ohio River on Route 2 can provide a perfect introduction to the area, before heading on a journey farther south.

The Route 2 drive officially starts in Chester and gets interesting pretty quickly. Just two miles out of Chester, in Newell, the Homer Laughlin China Company is a draw to china collectors from around the world. This ceramic company, founded in 1871, was the legendary producer of Fiesta, the colorful dinnerware started in 1936 that everyone covets today. The factory provides an interesting tour of the plant and process, as well as bargains at the retail factory outlet.

Continuing along Route 2 and the curves of the Ohio River, the road leads right through Weirton to the historic river town of Wellsburg. Founded in 1791, Wellsburg grew to become an important glass-foundry hub, with five large companies once based in the city. Brooke Glass Company is the only one left and it's going strong, with interesting tours providing details about the handmade products, and a retail gift shop.

Today, the town is a thriving tourist destination, with an historic district that boasts pre-Colonial, Federalist, and art deco styles of architecture, as well as wonderful co-op shopping at Watzman's Old Place. If you want to spend the night in historic Wellsburg, head for the Wellsburg Inn, with its lavish appointments, stained-glass windows, leaded-glass doors, hand-cut chandeliers, and a variety of guest rooms. Times Past Bed and Breakfast, the 1822 home of hosts David and Pam Cost, is another excellent option in town. The huge home-cooked buffets at Drover's Inn provide great meals in an 1848 inn.

Another town well worth visiting is Bethany, which is just six miles south of Wellsburg on Route 67. This pretty little town in the northern panhandle countryside is worth the diversion, with its quiet tree-lined streets, thriving Bethany College, and the Alexander Campbell Mansion serving as draws.

Bethany College was founded by leading businessman and scholar, Alexander Campbell, in 1840, and is known as one of the nation's top small liberal arts schools. Campbell had a profound influence on the development of Bethany and a tour of his mansion (built in the 1790s) provides an inside look at an earlier Bethany. The cemetery nearby is the burial ground for Campbell, many of his family members, and other Bethany dignitaries.

Back on Route 2, Wheeling is the next historic destination for the day (or night). If you can manage it, spend at least one night in Wheeling and stay at Oglebay Resort. This 1,500-acre complex began as Waddington Farm, the elegant summer estate of Cleveland industrialist Col. Earl W. Oglebay. In the late 1800s and early 1900s, the farm was one of the nation's premier agricultural centers, pioneering experimental farming techniques and heartier livestock breeds.

Upon his death in 1926, Oglebay willed his spectacular estate to the city of Wheeling for "as long as the people shall operate it for purposes of public recreation and education." The 750 acres became the varied Oglebay complex and his home became the Mansion Museum.

Since that time, under the imaginative direction of a nonpartisan board of philanthropic citizens, the resort has developed into a facility studied by planners nationwide as the only self-sustaining municipal park in operation today. The wide range of attractions and facilities draws visitors from across the nation.

The Wilson Lodge is the centerpiece of Oglebay Resort and the perfect place to end a country road drive. This spectacular facility, located on an impressive hilltop with stunning views, is crafted from fieldstone and wood. Features include fine dining and views in the Ihlenfeld Dining Room, the popular Glass Works Lounge, an indoor pool, and 36 cabins that are ideal for families to rent.

Other attractions at Oglebay include pretty Waddington Gardens, a re-creation of some of the gardens of old Waddington Farm; a huge outdoor pool; handcrafted glass at Carriage House Glass; the Mansion Museum; the 65-acre Good Children's Zoo; and some of the best golf in West Virginia.

If you can manage it, try to visit Oglebay Resort during the Winter Festival of Lights. This huge annual event (early November to early January, with varied opening times and days) is billed as "America's Largest Light Show" and it's easy to see why. More than 750,000 lights are spread over many miles, as the Oglebay landscape is blanketed with lights of all kinds—lighted trees, floodlit buildings and landscapes, and huge lighted displays. It's well worth a special trip. Special packages are available for the Winter Festival and throughout the year.

Oglebay Resort, as well as several local inns and B&Bs, can serve as an ideal base for exploring the rest of Wheeling. Just down the hill from Oglebay, be sure to stop by Stratford Springs for a meal (or a special night). This mini-resort has three suites and three guest rooms, as well as five gift shops on the premises. Listed in the *National Register of Historic Places*, the Stratford Inn provides first-class accommodations, lots of recreation facilities, and award-winning cuisine in seven separate dining areas.

While in Wheeling, visitors have the opportunity to take a Victorian homes tour, complete with all the memories of a bygone era. Elaborate architecture and intricately patterned stained glass impress everyone with their unsurpassed craftsmanship. Most impressive is that all materials used to build and decorate these homes were manufactured in Wheeling. Guided tours by the Wheeling Landmarks Foundation are usually available from April to January.

Elsewhere in Wheeling, be sure to check the schedule at Capitol Music Hall. Visitors can often catch a live country music performance by top-name entertainers where the country music radio show, "Jamboree USA," is broadcast live every Saturday night.

Just south of Wheeling, Moundsville makes for an interesting stop. This historic part of West Virginia once served as a spacious hunting and trading area for a much earlier generation of West Virginians. A prehistoric group called the Adena lived in the area around Moundsville from 1000 B.C. to about 200 A.D., and the area offers several reminders of their presence. The Adenas became known as "mound builders" because of their methods of burying their dead in huge mounds of earth. They built mounds generally ranging in size from 20 to 300 feet in diameter. They had well-organized societies living in a wide area, including much of present-day West Virginia, Ohio, Indiana, Kentucky, and parts of Pennsylvania and New York.

The largest example of Adena culture can be found at Moundsville's Grave Creek Mound State Park, which serves as the start of a leisurely drive on Route 250 across the state from the northern panhandle through Mountaineer Country to the Potomac highlands and the Virginia state line.

Grave Creek Mound State Park is one of the most unusual parks in a state full of unique state and federal parks. Easily found at 801 Jefferson Avenue in downtown Moundsville, the mound measures 295 feet at the base and 69 feet in height. Experts say the mound would have taken more than 100 years to complete and that the mound builders would have needed to remove 60,000 tons of dirt by hand.

Excavation of the mound required two shafts, one vertical and one horizontal, to gain access to the mound. Exploration revealed two burial vaults containing remains, Adena ornaments, and a small inscribed sandstone tablet.

Along with a quick climb to the top of the mound, the Delf Norona Museum at the base provides a good overview of the Adena period and lifestyle. The state penitentiary just across the street provides inmates for the upkeep of the park.

South of Moundsville, Route 2 continues winding along, parallel to the meandering Ohio River and lots of river-based industry. The views, along with a few small towns, make the miles pass quickly.

About 23 miles after leaving Moundsville, you'll drive straight through the glass-oriented town of New Martinsville. Be sure to follow the signs for Dalzell-Viking Glass, a company noted for its ruby-colored glass pieces.

Just 10 miles after New Martinsville, take a break in the small town of Sistersville. This pretty town is a perfect spot to stop for a bite to eat at the historic Wells Inn or for some unique shopping at the Townhouse Gallery at 718 Main Street. The Wells Inn features an old-world atmosphere and some of the region's best continental cuisine. Nearby, the Townhouse Gallery, located in a Victorian home in Sistersville's historic district, offers an "wholistic approach to art" and a wide range of art forms. The Sistersville national historic district features many large and pretty Victorian buildings, hinting at the oil and gas boom of the late 1800s.

Route 2 continues along the Ohio River and the parallel train tracks all the way into Parkersburg. For a short diversion before heading into Parkersburg for a visit or the night, take Route 31 over to Williamstown.

Williamstown's Fenton Art Glass Company has been in operation since 1905 and offers one of the best tours in the state. The factory tour, as well as a museum and large gift shop, make Williamstown an easy diversion for anyone interested in West Virginia's glassy past and present.

Rather than heading back to Route 2 for the drive into Parkersburg, you may want to take Route 14 south toward the city and then follow the signs for the Henderson Hall historic district.

This incredible complex is highlighted by Henderson Hall, a pre–Civil War mansion in the Italianate villa style. It is the only example of this style left in West Virginia and is furnished with original antiques. The guided tours of the house, with room after room of interesting furniture and memorabilia (including letters from Robert E. Lee) are worth a diversion before a push into Parkersburg.

The thriving river city of Parkersburg is a perfect place to spend a few hours, the night, or an entire weekend. Your first stop should be at the Parkersburg Visitors & Convention Bureau at 215 First Street, where you'll find a wide range of brochures concerning the history and culture of Parkersburg, as well as helpful personnel who are rightfully proud of their city.

If you're spending the night, your second stop should be the Blennerhassett Hotel. Truly one of the state's greatest hotels, the Blennerhassett has been open since 1889 and exudes the captivating atmosphere of the gaslight era. The hotel is registered as a National Historic Landmark and features rich crown moldings, authentic English doors, brass and leaded-glass chandeliers, and antiques hand delivered from England.

There are 104 spacious and pretty guest rooms in the hotel, which was restored in 1986. Award-winning Harman's Restaurant and the adjacent lounge also exude the elegance of another era. Quite simply, the Blennerhassett is the perfect Parkersburg base.

The Blennerhassett Hotel is named for one of the most famous families in West Virginia. Harman and Margaret Blennerhassett, originally members of the Irish aristocracy, moved to the United States in 1796 and eventually built a huge mansion on an Ohio River island near what would become Parkersburg.

The Blennerhassetts thrived at their mansion and had three children. However, Harman met Aaron Burr in 1805 and became heavily involved in an ill-fated plot to build an empire in the Southwest. The family eventually had to flee

Historic mansion on Blennerhassett Island

south to avoid arrest and spent the rest of their lives in poverty and failure.

Blennerhassett Island remained in complete disrepair until the 1970s, when the Blennerhassett Historical Park Commission began to protect the island. Burned to the ground in 1811, the Blennerhassett Mansion was perfectly reconstructed in the 1980s. Today Blennerhassett Historical State Park is one of America's most interesting island outings.

Ferries for the Blennerhassett complex depart from downtown's Point Park for the pretty 20-minute ride every half hour in season (typically late May through the last weekend of October). If you're hungry, grab a bite to eat and some great Ohio River views at the Point of View Restaurant.

The island's antiquity spans back to Ice Age hunters 9,000 years ago. American Indian tribes lived on the island almost continuously until White settlers forced them out, and they left many artifacts behind for archaeologists to discover. Today, there's even more to see. Visitors to the island may enjoy a crafts village, an eighteenth-century reproduction flatboat, refreshment and souvenir shops, picnic shelters, rental bikes, and hiking trails with many natural wonders. A variety of options are available for touring the complex, including tours through the mansion guided by costumed volunteers, self-guided walking tours, and horse-drawn wagon rides around the island.

Back in downtown Parkersburg, the Blennerhassett Museum is also part of the state park. Located at Second and Juliana Streets, this fascinating museum features three floors of exhibits and artifacts concerning the Blennerhassetts and the Parkersburg area. A 12-minute video provides more insight into the Blennerhassett legend.

The rest of Parkersburg is just as interesting. Book lovers should head straight for Trans Allegheny Books, one of the state's (and the region's) finest bookstores. Located in the old Carnegie Public Library at 725 Green Street, Trans Allegheny Books features thousands of used and new books. It's the perfect place to find many West Virginia titles, as well as hard-to-find, out-of-print books. Plan on spending several hours at this book mecca or at the store's other location in Charleston (see Chapter 3).

There are many other historic highlights in Parkersburg, including the Oil & Gas Museum (artifacts from the 1830s oil and gas boom); the Cook House (guided tours of an early 1800s home); the Smoot Theatre (a classic theater that now produces a stage show about the Blennerhassetts); and shopping at the Little Kanawha Craft House (locally produced items from more than 600 craftsmen).

If you spend the night at the Blennerhassett Hotel (and you should), eat at least one meal at Colombo's Restaurant, surely one of West Virginia's best dining choices. James B. Colombo started in the restaurant business in 1932 and moved to his present site in 1954. His friendly son, Jimmy, now runs this fascinating piece of Parkersburg history, but Mr. Colombo and his wife, Anna, are still there every day.

The restaurant features pasta and other Italian specialties, but there's so much more than just a tasty meal at Colombo's. The walls are filled with pictures of previous visitors and there's even a special Policeman's Room to honor those who served on the force. It's a Parkersburg experience that shouldn't be missed.

The rest of the drive down to Huntington can't match the interesting opportunities in Parkersburg, but Point Pleasant makes for a pleasant goal along the way. Route 2 joins I-77 until Ravenswood and you can take I-77 or Route 68 and then rejoin Route 2 in Ravenswood. There's really not much to see either way.

Take Route 2 for the 30-mile drive to Point Pleasant, where the Kanawha and Ohio Rivers converge at the site of the first battle of the American Revolution in 1774. The fight, when the colonists defeated Indians led by Shawnee Chief Cornstalk, kept the Indians from joining the British. It is commemorated at Point Pleasant Battle Monument State Park with a tall obelisk monument and many small memorials. There is also a restored log house on the grounds.

The West Virginia State Farm Museum is another interesting reason for stopping in Point Pleasant. Located just six miles north of town on Route 62, this living farm museum encompasses more than 50 acres, with 31 reconstructed buildings, including a log cabin, country store, blacksmith shop, schoolhouse, and church. The Farm Museum was a labor of love for Walden F. Roush, a retired educator who realized the need to preserve West Virginia's farming heritage.

You also shouldn't miss General, a mounted Belgian gelding that is the third largest horse on record. There's also a barnyard with farm animals, and a country kitchen that can prepare a cornbread and bean lunch with prior notice. Everything here provides a glimpse into the life of early farm families.

If you'd like to spend a pleasing night in quiet Point Pleasant, call the Stone Manor Bed and Breakfast on Main Street. Built in 1885 by the Stone family, this riverfront house was the base for the family's ferry business across to Ohio. Thomas and Janice Vance make for interesting and friendly hosts.

Heading south out of Point Pleasant, Route 2 crosses the Kanawha and hugs the Ohio River for the rest of the drive into Huntington, a great place to head for the night and the start or end of another West Virginia country road (see Chapters 3 or 4).

Huntington sits on the midsection of the scenic and historic Ohio River at the point where West Virginia, Ohio, and Kentucky meet. The city is home to more than 60,000 residents and serves a tri-state area of 365,000 people.

Huntington was named for its founder, Collis P. Huntington, who was builder, owner, and operator of the C&O Railway, which began in the 1860s. Huntington was known as "the Great Persuader" because of his aptitude as a natural-born salesman. In 1884, he became the first man in the United States to ride his own railroad car from the Atlantic Ocean to the Pacific over tracks he either owned or controlled.

Except for a few farms, mills, and a small college, what is now Huntington was undeveloped wilderness in 1869. Collis P. Huntington chose to build the city to serve as the western terminus of the transcontinental railroad because of nearby timber tracts, coal fields, oil, natural gas, and connections with Cincinnati by the Ohio River Steamboat. Thus, Huntington is one of the few cities that was planned logically, rather than just springing up haphazardly. The city was designed with tree-lined avenues 100 feet wide, and the railway was designed to run through town for easy access.

Huntington has developed into a bustling city that is an ideal residential and industrial hub for the Ohio River Valley. Consequently, there is much to see and do before heading east on Route 60.

For an overview of the city and its ties to the Ohio River, take a tour aboard the Jewel City Sternwheeler. It's like a country road drive on the water. Offering daily narrated one-hour tours and dinner cruises from April through October, the Jewel City features panoramic views and an historic atmosphere on a genuine sternwheeler.

Huntington is also the base for another type of tour excursion. The Collis P. Huntington Railroad Historical Society hosts fall foliage trips into the New River Gorge by steam train. The all-day affairs are an ideal way to see the area. The society also arranges other steam-train excursions from Huntington.

One of the city's top attractions is the Huntington Museum of Art. Opened in 1952, the museum is West Virginia's largest, providing residents and visitors access to distinguished collections, outstanding exhibitions, and nationally acclaimed educational programs. It is located on a pretty 50-acre hilltop site.

The museum collections reveal an exceptional range of artistic interests: American and European paintings, Oriental prayer rugs, Georgian silver, antique firearms, contemporary prints, and Appalachian folk art. One major strength is the Daywood Collection of American and European paintings, prints, and bronzes from the nineteenth and early twentieth centuries. The museum also houses many fine works of American furniture and decorative arts, as well as contemporary sculptures that are displayed indoors and in the outdoor sculpture-garden courtyard.

Back down the hill from the museum, Ritter Park serves as a peaceful country road getaway right in the middle of Huntington. The lovely 50-acre park stretches almost the entire length of the city. The park offers miles of tree-lined paths, tennis courts, picnic shelters, an open-air amphitheater, and one of the most beautiful rose gardens in the region.

The Museum of Radio & Technology is another interesting museum stop, providing a unique journey through time. From its inception, radio has played one of the most important roles in the technology explosion of the twentieth century. Located at 1640 Florence Avenue, the museum features a wide array of exhibits, including a parts store and service shop, classroom, radio communications room, library, supply room, radio center, and gift shop. If you are fascinated with radios and technology, this is a special treat.

Back in the center of the city, Huntington is very much a college town. Named for former U.S. Supreme Court Chief Justice John Marshall, Marshall University is the second largest state-supported university in West Virginia (behind West Virginia University). The school has grown from a small log building in 1837 to a university with more than 12,000 students on 60 acres of wooded land right in the city.

From the restaurants to the bars, the flavor of a college town can be seen everywhere downtown. One favorite spot is Heritage Village, located at the former B&O Railway Station at the corner of Eleventh Street and Veterans Memorial Boulevard. This award-winning complex contains an attractive plaza, unique shops, an authentic steam locomotive, a renovated Pullman car, and a statue of Collis P. Huntington.

Heritage Village also contains the famed Station Restaurant, which is worth visiting for lunch or dinner. Railroad memorabilia sets the mood for casual dining in rooms filled with history and railroad treasures. The burgers and French onion soup are justifiably popular. Rebels & Redcoats Tavern and Oliver's are two other excellent downtown dining choices.

If you plan to spend the night in Huntington after finishing the drive or before setting out the other way or on Route 60 (see Chapter 3), there are a wide variety of hotels downtown and on the eastern outskirts along Route 60. Some popular picks include: the sporty Coach's Inn or the Radisson Hotel downtown, or the small Colonial Inn or the Ramada Inn on Route 60.

In the Area

Homer Laughlin China Company (Newell): (304) 387-1300 or (800) 452-4462

Wellsburg Chamber of Commerce: (304) 737-2787

Brooke Glass Company (Wellsburg): (304) 737-3461

Watzman's Old Place (Wellsburg): (304) 737-0711

Wellsburg Inn: (304) 737-2751

Times Past Bed and Breakfast (Wellsburg): (304) 737-0592

Drover's Inn (Wellsburg): (304) 737-0188

Bethany historic district: (304) 829-7285

Alexander Campbell Mansion (Bethany): (304) 829-7285

Wheeling Convention & Visitors Bureau: (304) 233-7709 or (800) 828-3097

Oglebay Resort (Wheeling): (304) 243-4000 or (800) 624-6988

Stratford Springs (Wheeling): (304) 233-5100 or (800) 521-8435

Wheeling Landmarks Foundation: (304) 232-6400

Capitol Music Hall (Wheeling): (304) 234-0050 or (800) 624-5464

Grave Creek Mound State Park (Moundsville): (304) 843-1410 or (800) CALL WVA

Dalzell-Viking Glass (New Martinsville): (304) 455-2900

Wells Inn (Sistersville): (304) 652-1312

Townhouse Gallery (Sistersville): (304) 652-1214

Fenton Art Glass Company (Williamstown): (304) 375-7772 or (304) 295-4772

Henderson Hall historic district (Boaz): (304) 375-2129

Parkersburg Visitors & Convention Bureau: (304) 428-1130 or (800) 752-4982

Blennerhassett Hotel (Parkersburg): (304) 422-3131 or (800) 262-2536

Blennerhassett Historical State Park (Parkersburg): (304) 428-3000 or (800) CALL WVA

Point of View Restaurant (Parkersburg): (304) 863-3366

Blennerhassett Museum (Parkersburg): (304) 428-3000

Trans Allegheny Books (Parkersburg): (304) 422-4499

Oil & Gas Museum (Parkersburg): (304) 485-5446

Cook House (Parkersburg): (304) 422-6961

Smoot Theatre (Parkersburg): (304) 428-1130 or (800) 752-4982

Little Kanawha Craft House (Parkersburg): (304) 485-3149

Colombo's Restaurant (Parkersburg): (304) 428-9370

Point Pleasant Battle Monument State Park: (304) 675-3330

West Virginia State Farm Museum (Point Pleasant): (304) 675-5737

Stone Manor Bed and Breakfast (Point Pleasant): (304) 675-3442

Cabell Huntington Convention & Visitors Bureau: (304) 525-7333 or (800) 635-6329

Jewel City Sternwheeler (Huntington): (304) 453-5544

Collis P. Huntington Railroad Historical Society (Kenova): (304) 453-1641

Huntington Museum of Art: (304) 529-2701

Ritter Park (Huntington): (304) 696-5954

Museum of Radio & Technology (Huntington): (304) 525-8890

Marshall University (Huntington): (304) 696-3170 or (800) 642-3463

Station Restaurant (Huntington): (304) 523-6373

Rebels & Redcoats Tavern (Huntington): (304) 523-8829

Oliver's (Huntington): (304) 522-2415

Coach's Inn (Huntington): (304) 529-2761

Radisson Hotel (Huntington): (304) 525-1001 or (800) 333-3333

Colonial Inn (Huntington): (304) 736-3466

Ramada Inn (Huntington): (304) 736-3451 or (800) 228-2828

2

From the Northern Panhandle to the Potomac Highlands

Getting there: From Charleston, take I-79 north and I-70 west to Route 250 south for the start of the drive in Moundsville. You can also start the drive at the other end by heading to the Virginia border on Route 250.

Highlights: Prabhupada's Palace of Gold, Fairmont, a diversion to Morgantown or Clarksburg, the International Mother's Day Shrine in Grafton, Tygart Lake State Park and Tygart Dam, Philippi, Elkins, Helvetia, the Cheat Mountain Club, and the Monongahela National Forest. This drive is easily completed in two or three days, with overnight stays along the way or in Wheeling (see Chapter 1) at the start or end of the drive.

Though it's greatly influenced by the Ohio River and the neighboring states of Ohio and Pennsylvania, the northern panhandle is still very much West Virginia. A drive along the Ohio River on Route 2 (see Chapter 1) can provide a perfect introduction to the area, before heading on a journey across the state on Route 250. You may even want to

spend the night in Wheeling before setting
out on your journey from Moundsville (see
Chapter 1).

Take Route 250 out of Moundsville for
the start of the drive. A curvy and steep climb
provides an introduction to the country road driving ahead.
About 10 miles out of Moundsville, look for the left-hand
turn to the Palace of Gold. A winding road leads four miles
into the hills for this unique experience that should not be
missed. You round one final curve on the road to behold a
giant gold palace gleaming in the distance. Dubbed "America's
Taj Majal" by the *New York Times*, the Palace of Gold is a
huge temple constructed in the 1970s by a devoted band of the
New Vrindaban Spiritual Community, an offshoot of the Hare
Krishna movement founded in the 1960s by Srila Prabhupada.

A guided tour of the 10-room memorial to Prabhupada
features elaborate decoration, including more than 40 types of
imported marble and onyx. After you remove your shoes, the
interesting tour, guided by believers, includes an educational
video presentation and an inside look at all of the shimmer-
ing rooms.

The grounds feature stunning gardens (in season) and lots
of peaceful walkways and fountains. You'll often hear the
strains of religious music and chanting in the distance. If
you're hungry, you can even enjoy a vegetarian meal in the
Imperial Elephant Restaurant.

The grounds also include a large, and evidently popular,
conference center, where ceremonies and programs are held
throughout the day. You'll find the entire experience interesting, overwhelming, and certainly thought provoking.

Take the road back to Route 250 and continue on the
drive toward Fairmont. The next 30 miles before Mannington
feature lots of twists and turns in the road and plenty of
pretty vistas.

Mannington's claim to fame is the Round Barn, a completely circular barn built in 1912 to house cows, hay, and a farmer's family. Today, the Round Barn houses three floors of twentieth-century farm exhibits, early coal-mining tools, and other artifacts. The barn was originally heated by natural gas located directly on the farmer's land.

Follow the signs for the Round Barn in Mannington, as well as the West Augusta Historical Society Museum, with highlights including antique musical instruments; the original bed, chair, and dresser of the first governor of West Virginia; and an eclectic collection of area artifacts. The museum is located in an old brick schoolhouse, also built in 1912.

Route 250 heads farther south into Fairmont, another town of historical interest. History buffs will want to head straight for the Marion County Historical Society Museum, located downtown on Adams Street next to the courthouse. Built in 1897, it represents one of the finest examples of beaux arts classicism in West Virginia.

If you start on the third floor, the museum is arranged chronologically to depict different periods in U.S. history, with furnishings and artifacts of those times. Among many fascinating exhibits, highlights include lots of period toys, model railroads, and wartime artifacts.

More wartime history can be experienced at close range at Prickett's Fort State Park, just two miles north of Fairmont on I-79. Open from mid-April to late October, this park provides living history and much more.

Marion County's Prickett's Fort served as a refuge for earlier settlers, protecting them from attacks by Indians from 1774 to 1799. It was situated on the property of one of the earliest settlers, Jacob Prickett. He and his family, along with as many as 100 other families (up to 1,000 people), would use the fort often.

The park is devoted to depicting the life of early settlers in what was then Colonial Virginia. Depending on the time of year, visitors will find a wide variety of displays and demonstrations. It's best to check the schedule and displays at the Prickett's Fort Visitor Center.

The Meeting House is always active, with historical interpreters demonstrating the daily life of the settlers. The activities on the grounds include food preparation, blacksmithing, weaving, etc. Special events include an outdoor music weekend in the spring, summer encampment demonstrations, an apple butter weekend in the fall, and an eighteenth-century Christmas market in December. The McTrail ("Mc" for Marion County) leads walkers, joggers, and bikers two and a half miles from the park back to Fairmont, including a trip through a lit tunnel.

If you have time, head 15 miles north on I-79 for a look at lively Morgantown, West Virginia's big-time university town. West Virginia University sets the tone for this quaint college town, providing an eclectic mix of history, shopping, culture, WVU Mountaineer students, and high-tech education and research facilities. Though country roads provide the best transportation, Morgantown's Personal Rapid Transit System provides monorail-type twenty-first-century public transportation around the town and university. It's worth the trip for students and students at heart.

Some Morgantown highlights include the historic downtown area (great for stretching your legs), the WVA campus, the Old Stone House, and the Forks of Cheat Winery. This is also a great place to spend the night before heading farther on Route 250. One heavenly place is Almost Heaven B&B. For food and drink, the West Virginia theme can continue at the West Virginia Brewing Company.

In the other direction, Clarksburg makes for another interesting diversion off Route 250. The birthplace of Gen. Thomas "Stonewall" Jackson, Clarksburg's downtown historical district includes a wide variety of architectural styles, a huge bronze statue of Jackson on his horse, and a sculpture representing the many immigrants that flocked to the area in the late 1800s. Clarksburg is also a good place to stop for the night, with the cozy Main Street Bed and Breakfast making for an ideal spot.

Back on Route 250, the road from Fairmont leads to Grafton and an interesting landmark. Head into Grafton's downtown area and follow the signs to the International Mother's Day Shrine.

In 1908, Grafton resident Anna Jarvis organized a service to honor her mother and announced that she planned to promote a national mother's day. The first service was held in Grafton's historic Andrews Methodist Church, which now serves as the International Mother's Day Shrine and welcomes daily visitors.

Anna Jarvis is credited with promoting Mother's Day as a national holiday. Her birthplace can be seen four miles farther on Route 250 in Webster on the right-hand side.

Grafton is also the base for heading into Tygart Lake State Park, one of the state's finest recreation areas. Tygart Lake was formed by the construction of imposing Tygart Dam in 1938, leading to better flood control and a host of recreation possibilities. Take a look at the dam before heading into the park (tours are available on Wednesdays).

Tygart Lake State Park provides a huge array of water- and land-oriented recreation possibilities. The options include boating, swimming, fishing, scuba diving, hiking, and camping, with golf nearby. Visitors can enjoy the park for the day or they can stay at the 20-room lodge or in one of the 10 deluxe cabins in the woods.

The Tygart River, along with the Cheat River to the west, provides some of the popular and awe-inspiring white-water rafting trips that have made West Virginia famous (see Chapter 3 for information on white-water rafting the New and Gauley Rivers). For information on outfitters running trips on the Tygart or Cheat, call (800) CALL WVA. You'll experience a part of Mountaineer Country that even a country road can't help you explore.

The town of Philippi provides the next point of interest along Route 250, and you can literally take the country road right through this covered bridge. Though West Virginia had almost 90 covered bridges in the 1940s, Philippi's covered bridge is one of only 17 still standing in some form throughout the state.

Covered bridges provide a special treat for country road drivers and West Virginia has many fine examples. Bridges were originally covered to protect the wooden truss system of the road crossing the body of water. They were sources of great craftsmanship and architecture until iron railroad bridges made them obsolete. Finding a covered bridge down a country road in West Virginia is a true treat.

The Philippi covered bridge is the longest two-lane covered bridge still in use on a federal highway. It was erected in 1852 and served the North and South during the Civil War. Turn right into the parking area as soon as you exit the bridge for a closer look at this throwback to earlier country road driving. As with almost all covered bridges, this one makes for a great picture.

Another 30 minutes of winding country road driving takes you into the pretty college town of Elkins, the largest city in the Potomac highlands. Elkins has grown into a well-known community of artists, musicians, writers, and craftspeople.

The cultural scene in Elkins revolves around Davis and Elkins College. Founded in 1904, this small liberal arts campus has a big reputation to go along with its 900 students. The grounds and friendly students make for a great way to stretch your legs after some winding country road driving.

One of the best things about Davis and Elkins College grounds is Graceland Inn & Conference Center. Built in 1893 by Sen. Henry Gassaway Davis, one of the state's wealthiest coal and railroad barons, this magnificent example of Queen Anne–style architecture features 13 guest rooms furnished with distinctive period pieces to re-create the original Victorian elegance. There are also several suites, a conference center, a great hall, and a restaurant.

Davis and Elkins College is also the host site for the Augusta Heritage Arts Workshops, held each summer for five weeks beginning in July. These workshops provide in-depth exposure to the world's traditional arts, crafts, and music. The three-day grand finale features the popular Augusta Heritage Festival. In October, Elkins plays host to the 10-day Mountain State Forest Festival, the largest festival in the state, with the best of mountain arts, crafts, sports, music, parades, and woodchopping contests.

Depending on the time, Elkins may be a good spot to spend the night. Some quaint options include Graceland Inn & Conference Center, Wayside Inn B&B, the Post House, and Tunnel Mountain Bed & Breakfast. One larger option for accommodations or a good meal is the Elkins Motor Lodge.

Elkins also serves as a gateway for adventures in the Monongahela National Forest. This huge woodland area encompasses more than 901,000 acres of scenic mountains and forests. Some of the state's best fishing, hunting, and hiking can be found in this national forest. Much of this area, including the Canaan Valley, is covered in Chapter 7.

Begun in 1915 with the purchase of 7,200 acres, the Monongahela formally became a national forest in 1920. The lands purchased by the federal government for the forest had mostly been forested during the late 1800s and early 1900s and were often little more than bare hillsides. The early days of the Monongahela saw the reestablishment of a tree cover through planting programs. The Civilian Conservation Corps was active in the 1930s, building stone and timber pavilions and many other structures that remain today.

The Monongahela has expanded greatly since those early days and has regrown a thick new cover of trees. The forest is now able to support managed timber harvests, along with grazing and mineral programs, remote and highly developed recreation opportunities, and habitat for many species of wildlife.

The Allegheny front of the Appalachian Mountains forms the character of the area. The moist western side of the front contains northern hardwoods, such as cherry and maple, mixed with oak on the drier ridges and yellow poplar in the coves. The drier eastern side contains oak, cedar, and even cactus.

The mountains are also shaped by moving water, with the area home to the headwaters of five major river systems and hundreds of miles of smaller streams. These bodies of water mean good fishing, canoeing, and white-water rafting. Other recreational opportunities available to the visitor include camping (primitive and developed), bird-watching, rock climbing, hiking, caving, hunting, cross-country skiing, and much more.

After passing through Beverly, Dailey, and Valley Bend, slow down in Mill Creek for the right-hand turn to Helvetia on Route 46 west. This country road will take you on a winding journey to another era.

The tiny and isolated village of Helvetia seems much like it must have been in 1869 when it was founded by Swiss settlers. The small town now has few buildings and few permanent residents, but they welcome the many tourists who have heard about this interesting blend of alpine and Appalachian heritage.

Highlights of the Helvetia historic district include the church, a one-room schoolhouse, a museum, a restaurant, a small bed and breakfast, and lots of charm. It's well worth the 20-mile diversion off Route 250.

Huttonsville is just a few miles down the road from Mill Creek, once you're back on Route 250. Church services are still held in Huttonsville's 1883 Tygart Valley Church. The Hutton House Bed & Breakfast, an historic Queen Anne Victorian home, also offers a picturesque place to spend the night. If it's full, try Mr. Richard's Old Country Inn nearby.

Route 219 (see Chapter 6) splits off from Route 250 in Huttonsville, and the rest of the drive to the Virginia state line is all within the boundaries of the rugged Monongahela National Forest. If you have time (or can make time), the Cheat Mountain Club, located on the right just past Cheat Bridge, offers a perfect base for exploring this wilderness area.

The Cheat Mountain Club is a perfect mountain retreat for country road drivers. More than a century ago, members of the Cheat Mountain Sportsmen's Association built this large lodge for hunting and other mountain recreation, and it has since evolved into a special place for all to enjoy.

The large fireplace welcomes visitors to the hand-hewn, spruce-log interior of the lodge. Upstairs, there are seven double rooms, two single bedrooms, and a third-floor bunk room for children. Each room has a wash basin, while two spacious bath facilities are designated for male and female visitors.

The Cheat Mountain Club is located along the banks of the Shavers Fork River, one of West Virginia's finest trout streams, and surrounded by the huge Monongahela National Forest. As recorded in the club's historic guest register, the 180-acre private retreat was the lodging choice for Thomas Edison, Henry Ford, and Harvey Firestone during a 1918 visit to the state. Located just a mile away, the Cheat Mountain Outfitting and Guide Service is one of the state's most complete outdoor recreation companies, offering guided fishing trips with champion fisherman, Treve Painter, as well as hunting, hiking, mountain biking, and river running.

With so many outdoor activities, filling meals are a major event at Cheat Mountain Club. An experienced chef honors personal menu requests in preparing three family-style meals daily (served on the lodge's original china). Specialties include full-course country breakfasts, hearty soups and stews, home-baked breads and muffins, and bonfire picnics with all the trimmings.

Host Gladys Boehmer makes guests feel right at home at this unique retreat. It's simply a great place to end (or start) an exploration of West Virginia, from the northern panhandle to the highlands.

The rest of the drive leads over the Cheat Mountain summit to Durbin and then on to the Virginia state line.

In the Area

Grave Creek Mound State Park (Moundsville): (304) 843-1410 or (800) CALL WVA

the Palace of Gold (Vrindaban): (304) 843-1600

Round Barn (Mannington): (304) 986-2636

West Augusta Historical Society Museum (Mannington): (304) 986-2636

Marion County Historical Society Museum (Fairmont): (304) 367-5398

Prickett's Fort State Park (Fairmont): (304) 363-3030 or (800) CALL WVA

Greater Morgantown Convention & Visitors Bureau: (800) 458-7373 or (304) 292-5081

Personal Rapid Transit System (Morgantown): (304) 293-5011

WVu Visitors Center (Morgantown): (304) 293-3489

Old Stone House (Morgantown): (304) 296-7825

Forks of Cheat Winery (Morgantown): (304) 598-2019 or (304) 599-8660

Almost Heaven B&B (Morgantown): (304) 296-4007

West Virginia Brewing Company (Morgantown): (304) 296-2739

International Mother's Day Shrine (Grafton): (304) 265-1589

Tygart Lake State Park (Grafton): (304) 265-2320 or (800) CALL WVA

Tygart Dam (Grafton): (304) 265-1760

Philippi covered bridge: (304) 457-4846

Graceland Inn & Conference Center (Elkins): (800) 624-3157

Augusta Heritage Arts Workshops (Elkins): (304) 636-1903, ext. 209

Wayside Inn B&B (Elkins): (304) 636-6120

the Post House (Elkins): (304) 636-1792

Tunnel Mountain Bed & Breakfast (Elkins): (304) 636-1684

Elkins Motor Lodge (Elkins): (304) 636-1400

Monongahela National Forest (Elkins): (304) 636-1800

Helvetia historic district: (304) 924-6435

the Hutton House Bed & Breakfast (Huttonsville): (304) 335-6701

Mr. Richard's Old Country Inn (Huttonsville): (304) 335-6659

Cheat Mountain Club (Durbin): (304) 456-4627

Cheat Mountain Outfitting and Guide Service (Durbin): (304) 456-4073

3

Route 60 and the Midland Trail

Getting there: From Charleston, take I-64 west to the start of the drive in Huntington. You can also start the drive at the other end by heading to the Greenbrier on I-64 or Route 60.

Highlights: Huntington, Milton, Hurricane, St. Albans, Hamon Glass Studio, Charleston, Midland Trail Scenic Highway, Cabin Creek Quilts, Glen Ferris Inn, Hawks Nest State Park, New River Gorge National River, white-water rafting, Babcock State Park, the Greenbrier. This drive can be completed in two or three days, with overnight stays along the way or in Huntington or at the Greenbrier at the start or end of the drive. However, you should take the time for longer exploration, possibly breaking up your visit over several long weekends or a week or more of thorough exploration.

In many ways, Route 60 is the classic West Virginia road. It runs through large cities, large mountains, small towns, and small but interesting attractions. From big city life in Huntington to the capital, Charleston, and through the incredible countryside of the Midland Trail, Route 60 is one of West Virginia's best country road drives.

If you plan to spend the night in Huntington before setting out on Route 60, there are a wide variety of hotels downtown and on the eastern outskirts along Route 60. Some popular picks include the Coach's Inn and Radisson Hotel downtown, or the Colonial Inn and Ramada Inn on Route 60.

Once you set out on Route 60, you enter another West Virginia world. It doesn't take long for this world to begin unfolding.

The tiny town of Barboursville is just a few miles outside bustling Huntington. Located near the junction of the Mud and Guyandotte Rivers, the Barboursville area was a crossroads for Shawnee Indians. Hunting plentiful game and mining the salt nearby, the Indians (and lots of buffalo) established early and well-used trails. Today, the town's historic walking tour (map available from the Cabell Huntington Convention & Visitor's Bureau) features 36 points of interest, including homes, banks, businesses, and historic sites.

Just a few miles farther along on Route 60, be sure to stop at the town of Milton and the legendary Blenko Glass Visitor Center. The founder of Blenko Glass Company, William J. Blenko, came to America from London in the early 1890s for one purpose—to produce handblown glass for use in stained-glass windows. Blenko glass has been installed in St. Patrick's Cathedral in New York, Grant's Tomb, the Pro Football Hall of Fame, and the Washington Cathedral. In 1929, Blenko started producing handblown decorative glassware for such people as Eleanor Roosevelt and Mamie Eisenhower. Blenko glassware is now world famous.

Tours at Blenko are justifiably popular. From an observation platform, visitors can see the various steps in handcrafting glass: first, silica sand, combined with other materials, is fused under intense heat in a furnace; a gatherer takes a small portion of the fused material and blows it into a form or shape; a finisher completes the piece with handles, rings, or whatever is required; and the piece is gradually cooled to room temperature in an annealing oven.

After the tour, visitors can't resist the urge to visit the factory outlet. Upstairs, there's a stunning museum containing historical glass, information, and awards.

Milton is also the home of the Mountaineer Opry House. Generally running from October through May on Fridays and Saturdays, this family entertainment complex specializes in bluegrass and gospel music.

Another Milton attraction, near Blenko Glass, is the Mud River covered bridge. Near the junction of Route 25, just off Route 60, the pretty 112-foot bridge was built in 1876 and is still in use today.

If your visit to Blenko Glass is late in the day or you decide to attend a show at the Mountaineer Opry House, you should consider spending the night at Wine Cellar Bed & Breakfast. Hosts Susan and Bob Maslowski promise an interesting experience for guests. Susan is a potter and Bob is an archaeologist and home winemaker. You can enjoy both of their talents, as well as an inexpensive night in nice accommodations.

After leaving Milton and passing through Culloden, take Route 34 north for an easy one-mile diversion to the town of Hurricane. Legend has it that, in 1774, a party of surveyors commissioned by George Washington was traveling down the Kanawha River and noticed that all the trees at the mouth of a certain creek were bent in the same direction. They called the location "the place of the hurricane." The creek became known as Hurricane Creek, and by 1811, according to early Virginia maps, the town of Hurricane Bridge was located near where Route 34 now crosses the creek near Route 60.

Through the years, Hurricane Bridge became a stagecoach stop and a thriving livestock market center. In 1873, completion of a single-track railroad by Collis P. Huntington, connecting the Chesapeake and Ohio Rivers (a distance of 423 miles), resulted in the town being slightly relocated. The name was changed to Hurricane Station. The railroad caused the town to grow quickly, with the addition of hotels and stores, and in 1888, the town was incorporated as Hurricane.

Construction of I-64 during the 1960s gave Hurricane easy access to Charleston and Huntington, enabling the town to become an ideal location for people working in those cities. Today, Hurricane's downtown shops have been revitalized by the Downtown Hurricane Association. Specialty shops contain local and regional handmade arts and crafts, glass, fine antiques and collectibles, florals, and clothing.

As you stroll along Main Street, you'll find a lovely gazebo that's an ideal place to drop after you've shopped. It's easy to step back in time, imagining the way it was when Collis P. Huntington's railroad whizzed right through the town of Hurricane Station. If you time it right, you can even enjoy a home-style meal at one of Hurricane's many local restaurants.

Back on Route 60, after another eight miles, you'll enter the city of St. Albans. The big draw to this Charleston suburb is another legendary West Virginia restaurant. The Wren's Nest (call for directions) was established in 1926 in a log cabin located on the Coal River in a rural area near St. Albans.

Willard and Mattie Wren, when choosing a name for their little restaurant, added a birdhouse to their lamppost and named it the Wren's Nest Tea Room. Mattie Wren began serving meals in her home, then a larger dining room and kitchen were added when more and more people began coming to enjoy her home-cooked chicken dinner and cheese soufflé. Like most families of that time, the Wrens raised their own chickens. The specialty is still included on the menu today, but the chicken coop is gone.

When Mrs. Wren retired from her Tea Room in 1958, Reba Campbell bought and ran the restaurant for 26 years, adding her daughter and many other family members as helpers. In 1984, Reba's daughter and son-in-law, Janice and Ray Holley, as well as their two children, took over the Wren's Nest. Reba still helps out when needed. The Wren's Nest has always been family operated.

Ray, an avid collector of military and civilian uniforms from World War II to present day, added rooms to display his collection, as well as more dining space. He also added a dancing area and live music at the Stage Door Canteen, a supper club patterned after the USO canteens of the 1940s. The music is mostly from that time period, making for a nostalgic way to spend an evening.

The canteen also features Ray's collection of old newspapers, Uncle Sam posters, and many wartime artifacts from early conflicts all the way through Desert Storm.

A reputation for fine food continues at the Wren's Nest. Dinner is served leisurely in courses, with the longtime house specialties remaining secret recipes. Waitresses are dressed in apron uniforms similar to those worn by the Red Cross women of the 1940s. From the dancing to the decor to the food, it all combines to make for a unique Kanawha Valley evening.

While in St. Albans, West Virginia glass fans should also make a point to head north on Route 35 and then follow the signs (and many turns) leading to Hamon Glass Studio (just call if you get lost). This small husband-and-wife studio is much more intimate than many of the larger glass factories in West Virginia. Finding the perfect dazzling handblown paperweight by Robert and Veronica Hamon in their gift shop may be the highlight of your Route 60 drive.

Route 60 leads toward Charleston and another capital West Virginia city experience that still has lots of country charm. The first stop is actually South Charleston, which sits to the south of the city across the Kanawha River.

South Charleston is the site of the second largest remaining Adena Indian burial mound (see Chapter 1) in the state behind Grave Creek Mound State Park. It is located in the downtown business district along MacCorkle Avenue (Route 60), fronting Oakes Avenue and Seventh Avenue. The Mound is a large earthen pile measuring 175 feet in diameter at the base and approximately 35 feet high.

There are many existing mounds of various sizes in areas of West Virginia, Ohio, and Kentucky, although many have been destroyed by land developers. Most of the remaining mounds have been excavated by archaeological teams and the artifacts and remains have undergone meticulous study and interpretation. Skeletal analysis reveals that this primitive society of early mound builders was a broad-faced race of people who practiced the cultural custom of flattening and reshaping the head through the use of a cradle board in infancy. Charred bone fragments found in some mounds also indicate that cremation was performed.

Some scholars believe the Adena Indian civilization originally came from Mexico and Central America, by way of the Mississippi and Ohio Rivers, to the Kanawha Valley, while others feel they were descended from a people who crossed to this hemisphere from Europe.

The excavation of the Mound in South Charleston was performed by the Smithsonian Institution in 1883 and 1884. It revealed 13 complete skeletons and parts of another, a flint lancehead, copper bracelets, arrowheads, tools, and various metal and shell ornaments, which are now in the possession of the Smithsonian Institution in Washington, D.C. Some of the artifacts are on loan to the Sunrise Museum in Charleston.

Today, the Mound is a grass-covered hill stuck between urban and industrial growth. However, it's worth stopping to ponder an earlier and simpler time.

The Sunrise Museum, located up the hill on Myrtle Road

is actually made up of two mansions on each side of the road, overlooking the city across the river. The museum is the home of Children's Hands-on Museum of Charleston and the Charleston Art Gallery, making it enjoyable for all ages. Be sure to see the stone fireplace, which contains stones acquired from old structures around the world, including the Tower of London and the Great Wall of China.

Route 60 leads across the Kanawha River and into the heart of Charleston, surely one of the most interesting state capitals in the United States. You should plan on spending a day or more in this lovely city.

If you want a perfect base for exploring Charleston, call the Brass Pineapple Bed & Breakfast for reservations. Proprietress Sue Pepper has turned this lovely home into one of the finest bed and breakfasts in the state.

In 1907, Charleston real estate magnate E. C. Bauer and his wife, Clara, purchased a lot on what was then the outskirts of town. Although they owned lots of land in the county, they wanted this Virginia Avenue site for their home. By 1910, the house was completed with the finest materials of the day— matched oak paneling, Italian tilework, and an abundance of stained and leaded art nouveau and Victorian glass. After the original state capitol downtown burned to the ground in 1921, the new capitol was built just a quarter mile from the Bauer home.

This lovely old brick home was lovingly restored by Sue Pepper. The Brass Pineapple features six cozy guest rooms with central air and heat. Each is individually and stunningly appointed with antiques, cable television, phones, fluffy designer robes, soft linens, private baths, and much more.

Days begin with freshly ground coffee or tea and a choice of continental or full traditional breakfast. Breakfast is served in the elegant dining room, but can also be enjoyed alfresco on the veranda or in the petite-rose garden in warmer months.

A light afternoon tea is available weekends and may also

be enjoyed on the veranda during warmer months. The veranda is candlelit after dark. On chilly spring and fall nights, warm afghans and hot chocolate are added for extended enjoyment of this Victorian add-on. Evenings end with mints or custom chocolates left on pillows of turned-down beds.

You may not want to leave the Brass Pineapple, but there's much more to explore in the capital, literally right outside your front door.

The area that is now Charleston was actually occupied in the mid-1700s by fur traders, who peacefully coexisted with Shawnee, Cherokee, and Mingo Indians. In 1788, Virginians decided to build Fort Lee to protect themselves from increasing tension. The area outside the fort was originally named Charles Town and was even represented by Daniel Boone in the Virginia assembly. It was eventually renamed Charleston in 1819. The West Virginia state capitol and capitol complex should be your first stop, reached by heading a half block to your right from the front door of the Brass Pineapple.

West Virginia's majestic state capitol ranks among the nation's most significant examples of twentieth-century classical architecture. Designed by Cass Gilbert, architect of the U.S. Treasury annex and the U.S. Supreme Court building, the capitol holds an honored place in the history of the nation's architectural accomplishments as the last monumental capitol of renaissance design constructed in America.

West Virginia is the only state in the Union to have acquired its sovereignty by proclamation of the president of the United States. Statehood was given by President Abraham Lincoln in 1863, midway through the Civil War. Only seven years later, West Virginia's seat of government began traveling intermittently between Wheeling, site of the inauguration of the state's first governor, and Charleston, the final choice as the state capital.

Charleston was chosen as the state's capital by popular election in 1877. In 1885, the first capitol was opened and state officials and records were transferred from Wheeling by two steamers and a barge. The building was destroyed in 1921 and a new capitol was not completed and dedicated until 1932.

Encompassing more than 14 acres of floor space, the capitol is made of buff limestone over a steel frame. It is dominated by a dome 293 feet high, which is five feet higher than that of the U.S. Capitol. The building required more than 700 carloads of limestone and 160 carloads of steel weighing 4,640 tons.

Limestone pillars, each weighing 86 tons, support matching porticos at the north and south entrances. Beneath each portico are 2,800-pound brass and copper doors decorated with carved elm, hickory, beech, and maple leaves representing West Virginia's native hardwood trees. Gracing the east and west entrances are limestone heads of Greek and Roman deities, which were sculpted in place.

Two-thirds of the interior is made of Imperial Danby marble. The floors are a combination of dark Italian travertine and white Vermont marble. In the foyers outside the second-floor legislative chambers are 34-ton solid marble columns. Lining the hallway which separates the two chambers are smaller columns of black Belgian marble, one for each of West Virginia's 55 counties. The ceilings at the end of each hallway are hand carved from West Virginia wood in leaf designs, which also represent the state's hardwood trees.

Sheltered by the interior dome of the capitol, 180 feet above the ground floor, a 4,000-pound chandelier made of more than 3,300 pieces of hand-cut Czechoslovakian crystal hangs from the ceiling. It is eight feet in diameter and has a 54-foot gold-plated chain. Lighted only on special occasions, the chandelier is lowered by hand crank every four years and each piece of crystal is removed and cleaned for the governor's inauguration. A circular design on the floor has the same diameter as the chandelier above.

The capitol serves as the meeting place for the West Virginia legislature. The senate chamber houses 34 members in the west wing of the capitol, while 100 delegates meet in the house of delegates chamber in the east wing. Similar chandeliers of Czechoslovakian hand-cut crystal hang in each chamber, while every delegate and senator has a hand-carved walnut desk. Each chamber also displays a hand-carved cherry replica of the great seal of West Virginia, bearing the state motto, "Montani Semper Liberi"—Mountaineers Are Always Free.

Guided tours of the capitol are offered year-round, Monday through Saturday, with additional tours available on Sundays during the summer.

The state capitol houses more than 300 rooms, but is only the focal point of a much larger state capitol complex. Clusters of office buildings stand at the north, east, and west sides of the capitol, all linked by an attractively landscaped pedestrian mall which includes two picturesque fountains.

The spacious lawn allows impressive views of the capitol's mass and perfect proportion. At night, when the state capitol is bathed in light, attention is irresistibly drawn to the front entrance, where the imposing statue, *Lincoln Walks at Midnight*, is cast in shadow, reminding visitors of the turbulent birth of the 35th state.

Several other statues of significance grace the capitol grounds. A commanding statue of Stonewall Jackson on the southeastern corner salutes those who held Southern sympathies during the Civil War. On the northeastern corner, a Union mountaineer honors those of the home guard who protected the state from Southern incursion. On the southwestern corner, the representation of a Union soldier stands as a tribute to the 32,000 West Virginia soldiers who served the Union cause.

The bust of Booker T. Washington stands at the end of the west wing of the capitol. This renowned educator and advocate of interracial cooperation spent his early life in the town of Malden, where he taught for two years following his graduation from Virginia's Hampton Institute in 1875.

On the steps leading to the north portico of the capitol is a replica of the Liberty Bell. Identical to the original, it is one of 53 cast in France and given to the U.S. government.

In addition to the capitol building and the pretty grounds, the capitol complex includes the governor's mansion, the cultural center, and the West Virginia State Museum. All are well worth visiting for any fan of West Virginia.

During the first 30 years of statehood, the governor was required to furnish his own quarters. This changed in 1893, when the legislature provided funding for a house to be built and furnished. After the capitol burned and was relocated, funding for a new governor's mansion was provided.

The current governor's mansion, which overlooks the Kanawha River, was built in 1925. Gov. Ephraim Morgan was the first to occupy the mansion, one week before his term expired that same year.

Upon entering the mansion, a dual Georgian staircase presents a dramatic study in grace and symmetry, enhanced by the black Belgium- and white Tennessee-marble floor. Solid cut-crystal finials on the newel posts add elegance to the mahogany staircases. The entry portal and restored chandelier are Georgian.

The ground floor of the mansion houses the state rooms, including the ballroom, which features chandeliers that once hung in Scott's Drug Store on Capitol Street in Charleston; the dining room, which includes an 1820s banquet table that seats 22 guests; the drawing room, graced by chandeliers from the old Kanawha Hotel in Charleston and a lovely mantel that is a replica from the president's cottage at the Greenbrier; and the library, with Georgian-style butternut paneling that displays the quality of West Virginia hardwood. The second floor of the mansion serves as the private residence for the state's first family.

The cultural center is also a capital-area attraction. Opened in 1976, this interesting complex includes the West Virginia State Museum, arts and crafts by state residents, reference and archives libraries, and the state theater. The complex, managed by the West Virginia Division of Culture and History and the West Virginia Library Commission, is a wonderful asset for the state and visitors.

The great hall of the cultural center offers a changing variety of exhibits concerning West Virginia. The museum traces West Virginia's history from Indian times to present day with a huge collection of artifacts from throughout the state. If you can't visit every part of West Virginia on country roads, this is a fun alternative. The libraries feature thousands of volumes and other records about West Virginia, all for public use.

You may also want to ask about *Goldenseal*, a magazine covering West Virginia's folk life that is published by the museum.

The State Theater is the home of *Mountain Stage*, a popular radio program broadcast most Sundays to the rest of the country through public radio. If you're going to be in Charleston, call in advance about tickets for the taping.

Finally, be sure to stop by the complex shop. If you want a genuine West Virginia souvenir, this is the place to get it, with its wide variety of West Virginia arts and crafts.

Elsewhere in Charleston, the revitalized downtown area offers several interesting shopping diversions. The biggest is definitely Town Center Mall, one of the nation's largest downtown shopping malls. The oldest can be found at Hale Street Antiques and Collectibles Mall. But the best may be Trans Allegheny Books, the huge sister store of the famed bookshop in Parkersburg. If you like books, plan on spending many hours here.

The Charleston Convention & Visitors Bureau can provide a map of the downtown area that highlights many of the historic landmarks. Buildings of interest include the restored Capitol Theatre, the old Kanawha Hotel, city hall, the old Daniel Boone Hotel, Taylor Books (also great book shopping), and the C&O railroad depot just across the river.

If you do spend the night at the Brass Pineapple or elsewhere in Charleston, your hosts can provide several local dining possibilities in the downtown area. Cagney's is one of the most popular choices with Charleston residents.

Heading out of Charleston on Route 60, the Midland Trail Scenic Highway begins quickly as the downtown skyline disappears.

Stretching 120 curving miles along Route 60 from Charleston all the way to White Sulphur Springs, the Midland Trail is a road of West Virginia history that most visitors miss by taking speedier I-64. But those who slow down on Route 60 are richly rewarded.

Great herds of buffalo first beat this path across the southern Appalachian Mountains. Indians dragged captive Mary Draper Ingles across portions of it. Mad Anne Bailey rode the trail, while Daniel Boone walked it. Collis P. Huntington's railroad through the New River Gorge left the trail in the dust, until the automobile revived a need for it. Today, generations of history and ghosts haunt every mile, with 200 years of exploration, conquest, and American industrial history around every curve.

Though you can drive the route now in a few hours, a nineteenth-century stagecoach trip took at least two grueling days from the Kanawha Valley, over the Fayette Plateau and the New River Gorge, and into the Greenbrier River Valley.

As you're heading out of town, look for Daniel Boone

Park on the banks of the Kanawha River. Along with a picnic area and a playground, the park is the home of the Craik-Patton House, one of the area's finest historic homes. This fully restored house was built by James Craik in 1834 and then occupied by George Smith Patton, grandfather of five-star Gen. George S. Patton. Most of the rooms are furnished as they would have been in Craik's day, except for the Patton Room, which is furnished in the later style.

Just another few miles out of town, Malden is the first Midland Trail stop of interest. This town, originally known as Kanawha Salines thanks to huge salt production, has many claims to fame. After the Civil War, an adolescent Booker T. Washington, newly freed from slavery, came to Malden for work in the brines. The wife of an important salt magnate taught him to read and he went on to become an effective spokesman for Black Americans, as well as founder of the Tuskegee Institute. A park honoring him stands on the site of his sister's home, where he once lived and often visited.

Malden is also the home of Cabin Creek Quilts. Founded in 1970, this award-winning quilting cooperative features a wide array of handmade quilts on display and for sale. Visitors will also find handcrafted pillows, wall hangings, clothing, kitchen accessories, baby items, and much more at the bright pink house located right in Malden on Route 60.

After another six miles, in the small town of Belle, look for the Samuel Shrewsbury Sr. House (also called the Old Stone House). Built by Sam and his brother, John, in the early 1800s, this pretty little house features a hand-cut sandstone exterior and hand-hewn walnut woodwork inside. Though the beauty of the exterior is marred by a chemical plant in the background, the interior can be viewed with advance notice.

Route 60 curves its way along the Kanawha River and the parallel train tracks, with tiny towns and pretty scenery as the backdrop. The names of the towns—Smithers (an early settler), Cedar Grove, Boomer, and Alloy—reveal the influence of early homesteaders, timber, and precious metals on the area.

Be sure to stop in Glen Ferris, where the river roars over a high, jagged ledge to form the pretty Kanawha Falls. Known as Stockton until 1895, the town grew up around Col. Aaron Stockton's tavern, Stockton's Inn. Today, the tavern, registered in the *National Register of Historic Places*, is named the Glen Ferris Inn.

Opened in 1839 as a stagecoach stop alongside the scenic Kanawha Falls, the inn was owned by Stockton, a slave-owning farmer and coal entrepreneur. The inn was fired upon in 1861, as the Confederate Army fought for control of the South. The inn withstood the assault and continued to serve as home to travelers and army personnel during the War Between the States.

One of Stockton's grandchildren helped bring an end to stagecoach travel to the inn. Oscar Veazer completed surveying the New River Gorge for the C&O Railroad in 1869 and the resulting railroad opening diminished the stagecoach trade the inn had previously enjoyed.

In 1901, the rising interest in ferroalloys instigated the building of the Wilson Aluminum Plant, which later became part of Union Carbide Corporation. The company bought the inn from Margaret Hawkins Williamson for $100, added a building to house 10 additional guest rooms, and changed the name to the Glen Ferris Inn.

When the Norwegian company, Elkem, purchased Union Carbide's ferroalloys facilities in the United States, the Glen Ferris Inn became an international host for Norwegian guests. In 1991, Elkem returned the inn's hospitality by restoring the building's original historic charm. This renovation made the Glen Ferris Inn one of West Virginia's top getaways.

The inn's 15 guest rooms have each been decorated with distinct styles. From Queen Anne to Victorian to Shaker, guests can choose from a variety of time periods in which to sleep, bathe, and luxuriate. The cuisine matches the grandeur and uniqueness of the inn's decor. Diners can feast on quail and lobster tail, as well as fried apples and yeast rolls. You'll return to the Midland Trail having experienced an historic stay.

Just down the road from Glen Ferris sits the town of Gauley Bridge, hugging a steep corner of the mountain above the juncture of the New and Gauley Rivers, the pivotal point between the New River Gorge and the Kanawha Valley.

A man named Miller operated a ferry and tavern here until a toll bridge was built on the new Kanawha Turnpike in 1822. The bridge stood until 1826, when a fire attributed to "persons interested in the ferry" destroyed it.

A second bridge stood until the Civil War. In 1861, Confederate General Floyd yielded control of the Kanawha Valley at the bridge to Union General Rosecrans, but burned the bridge as a farewell gesture. Its mossy piers can still be seen.

As the Midland Trail winds its steep western ascent onto the Fayette Plateau, the mountains sometimes part, exposing dramatic views of the prehistoric, boulder-strewn New River hundreds of feet below. It's tough to keep your eyes on the winding road and you're often better off pulling over for better views.

Indian scout Mad Anne Bailey rode across this route for help in 1788, leaving a besieged fort on the Elk River and heading to Fort Savannah in Lewisburg. She confounded her Indian pursuers when, as legend has it, she rode her horse, Liverpool, off Hawks Nest cliff, saving the day and her scalp.

Hawks Nest State Park is one of the drive's most interesting stops and a great place to linger for a hike, a meal, the night, and much more.

The 276-acre park, one of the state's most popular, features incredible views of the New River Gorge, a 31-room lodge, a dining room with filling meals and views, and a seasonal aerial tramway that runs all the way to the marina at the

A view of the New River Gorge from Hawks Nest State Park, Ansted.

bottom of the gorge. Other activities include hiking, swimming, boating, tennis, and shopping for handmade West Virginia crafts in the lodge's shop.

The town of Ansted is just past the entrance to the park. In 1790, a group of Baptists formed a community here called New Hope. It was rechristened Ansted in 1861 in honor of an English coal speculator.

Confederate Col. George Imboden settled in Ansted after the Civil War to develop his Fayette County coal interests. He was the first mayor of Ansted. His home, Contentment, was built in the 1830s and features much original intricate woodwork. The grounds also include a museum devoted to Fayette County history and a restored one-room schoolhouse. Nearby

Westlake Cemetery is the final resting place for Stonewall Jackson's mother, Julia Neale Jackson.

Route 60 crosses Route 19 about 10 miles farther down the road. Fight the urge to head straight across the busy road to get back on peaceful Route 60. There's much to see and do around this intersection.

The first thing you should do is head south on Route 19 to the Canyon Rim Visitors Center, located near Lansing. Built in 1991, the modern visitors center features spectacular views of the New River Gorge inside and outside, as well as an interesting slide show, exhibits, shopping, hiking, and many programs.

The views of the 53-mile New River Gorge National River reveal the spectacular nature of this area, formed more than 65 million years ago by advancing glaciers. It has an average depth of more than 1,000 feet. A trip across the river that once took an hour now takes a minute.

You also get a great view of the New River Gorge Bridge. Built in 1977, the bridge is 3,030 feet long, making it the longest single-arch-span bridge in the world. It towers 876 feet above the New River and is the highest bridge east of the Mississippi. The bridge contains more than 42 million pounds of structural steel.

One of the best hiking areas here is the Mary Ingles Trail, which may have been used by Mary Draper Ingles when she made her famous escape from the Shawnee Indians. The three-mile trail features pretty views of Thurmond, a tiny town that once thrived on a booming coal economy—and the world's longest continuous poker game, which lasted more than 14 years.

If you happen to be in the area on the third Saturday in October, you shouldn't miss Bridge Day. The New River Gorge Bridge is closed to traffic on this day, when hundreds of base-jumping parachutists and rapellers take the plunge off it.

The area is also a perfect base for white-water rafting adventures. You can't say you've seen West Virginia if you haven't been white-water rafting.

West Virginia is fast becoming known as the Colorado of the East, and the white-water rivers are a big reason. Tourism is now one of the largest industries in the state and commercial white-water rafting plays a big part. West Virginia's rivers are practically one giant backyard playground. Each year, more than 250,000 people go white-water rafting in the state.

Rafting in West Virginia is made easy by the more than 25 outfitters operating on the state's major white-water rivers. Any commercial trip is just a phone call away. But the recent addition of all-inclusive packages with many companies has made white-water rafting even easier to arrange and enjoy.

Every outfitter in West Virginia is unique. Operations can vary from small buildings to elaborate base camps with stores, restaurants, campgrounds, and much more. Many companies offer popular, convenient, and discounted package arrangements, including rafting, accommodations, food, etc.

Class VI River Runners in Lansing, one of the state's most successful white-water companies, offers a number of great packages. This legendary company and its co-founder and co-owner, Dave Arnold, are typical of the businesses and people that are succeeding in West Virginia's tourism industry.

Class VI's base camp is north of Beckley in a 1,000-acre oak forest overlooking the New River Gorge, often called "the Grand Canyon of the East." Many outfitters that run the New and Gauley Rivers are based in this area.

Class VI's facilities include a check-in area, a large store, a highly recommended restaurant, rest rooms, and a viewing platform overlooking the stunning gorge. The check-in is well organized and paddlers move quickly to the bus and put-in.

Class VI's New River trip provides a perfect example of what to expect on a white-water trip in West Virginia. Each raft has a guide to explain everything needed to hit the river. After the quiet start, the rapids progress in difficulty and enjoyment. The gorge has an average width of one mile and the beauty of its ancient walls makes for spectacular sightseeing and some interesting history from the well-informed guides. The New River trip offers some large drops and plenty of excitement. Class VI stops along the banks of the river for an elaborate picnic lunch that includes many freshly prepared gourmet choices. The lunches are so popular that Class VI published a cookbook for all its loyal paddlers and diners.

More rapids follow after lunch, before a late-afternoon finish and a bus ride back to Class VI. Typical topics of conversation on the bus include the best rapids, the funniest guides, and the sheer beauty of the area.

The New River is the most popular choice for new as well as veteran rafters. The commercial season begins in March and lasts through November. Because of the length of season and the volume of water, the New receives more than 100,000 rafters each year. The calmer upper New is very popular for family packages.

The other major river in the Beckley area is the famed Gauley River. White-water rafters come from throughout the country to run this river each fall. The flow is controlled by Summersville Dam and it is typically open for commercial rafting trips on Fridays through Mondays in the fall.

Up north, near Morgantown (see Chapter 2), the Cheat and Tygart Rivers are the big draw. More than 50,000 people raft the Cheat (class III to V) each year, most of them going between early April and Memorial Day. The riverbed is littered with massive boulders, and it can be a great raft trip at any water level. The Tygart (class III to V) is less well-known, but its rapids are continuous and complex.

Those new to white-water rafting in West Virginia can

take advantage of popular packages. Class VI has many creative offerings and can arrange the logistics of an entire stay. You can just book a simple rafting trip, but you can also book camping, meals, B&B stays, mountain biking, horseback riding, specific trips for families and children, and other activities. Class VI even offers surprisingly convenient and reasonable air packages with USAirways, if you don't have time to take the Midland Trail.

There are many other outstanding outfitters in the area and throughout the state. For information, call (800) CALL WVA.

Fayetteville, just south of the river, has become the Durango of the East, with excellent outdoor shops, accommodations, and dining. It's an ideal base for mountain biking with Ridge Rider Mountain Bikes, a balloon ride through the gorge with New River Balloons, a night at the Morris Harvey House or the White Horse, or a creative meal at the funky Sedona Grill.

North of Route 60, on Route 19, the Summersville Lake area is another outdoor draw. Featuring more than 60 miles of shoreline, Summersville Lake was formed when the Summersville Dam was built to control the Gauley River (the fall releases create the Gauley white-water season).

The Army Corps of Engineers broke a long-standing tradition in naming the Summersville project. The Corps usually names a project after the town nearest the construction site. However, Gad, not Summersville, was the town closest to the site. The Corps decided not to call it Gad Dam and used the second-closest town for the name.

Along with boating, fishing, and swimming, crystal-clear Summersville Lake also offers great scuba diving. Lessons and gear are available from the friendly folks at Sarge's Dive Shop. The clear water, steep underwater cliffs, and catfish can make for an unusual West Virginia underwater experience.

If you're in the area and want an unusual West Virginia

culinary experience, call the Country Road Inn to see if Mama Jarroll has a table (be sure to get directions). With a name like "Country Road," you can't go wrong!

The Jarroll family's lovely old farmhouse nestled on a hillside is the setting for one of the state's most famous restaurants. The Country Road Inn features a wide array of Italian cuisine, all served family style, ranging from huge antipasto salads to a choice of entrees to the famed tortoni for dessert. The food is usually served by friendly family members, and a welcome at the door or tableside visit from Mama Jarroll is standard.

If you're just too full to go any farther, get a room at the Historic Brock House Bed and Breakfast Inn. Jim and Margie Martin are your hosts at this inn that has welcomed visitors for more than 100 years.

Back on Route 60, the drive isn't quite as exhilarating as white-water rafting, but it's still quite interesting. Look for Midland Trail Gallery at the junction of Routes 60 and 41. David Weaver moved to West Virginia from Alaska and has established an arts and crafts haven for his paintings, as well as the work of many other talented West Virginians. It's worth an extended stop to see his work and many other interesting pieces of art.

Take Route 41 south to Babcock State Park for another perfect West Virginia park experience. Along with rustic cabins and camping, the outdoor highlight of this park is Glade Creek Grist Mill. This pretty mill is surely one of the most photographed buildings in the state.

Back on Route 60, the winding road continues over towering Big Sewell Mountain to Rainelle, once the home of the world's largest hardwood mill, the Meadow River Lumber Company. The founding brothers, John and W. T. Raine, gave the town its name.

Route 60 intersects with I-64 near Sam Black Church,

which makes the trip west or east go much more quickly. However, it's not nearly as interesting.

After hours of winding along Route 60 and then paralleling I-64 for 10 miles, the town of Lewisburg provides a great place to rest for a few hours or days. Ideally situated at the intersection of Route 60 and Route 219 (see Chapter 6), Lewisburg is a perfect country road town.

The final stop on the Midland Trail is perhaps the best. The legendary Greenbrier is one of America's finest resorts and deserves a stay of several days, if at all possible.

Nathaniel Carpenter claimed 950 acres of Greenbrier Valley by planting corn in the mid-1750s. The local Shawnee hunting club responded by killing him and most of his family. In 1808, grandson-in-law James Calwell returned to the original stake and built a tavern, dining room, ballroom, and a row of cottages, drawing more visitors to the healing White Sulphur Springs.

These cottages eventually developed into a small resort, where, according to the Greenbrier brochure, the nation's elite came "each to throw his pebble on the great heap of general enjoyment." According to one 1834 account, the waters cured "yellow jaundice, white swelling, blue devils, and black plague . . . fever of every kind and color, hypochondria and hypocrisy, and bad habits except chewing, smoking, spitting, and swearing."

Today, the Greenbrier still heals weary travelers. With more than 6,500 acres, 700 luxurious rooms, charming cottages, elegant appointments and service, creative dining, a top-notch spa, world-class golf, tennis, horseback riding, and much more, it has everything any West Virginia visitor could want. It's the perfect way to end (or start) another great West Virginia country road drive.

In the Area

Coach's Inn (Huntington): (304) 529-2761

Radisson Hotel (Huntington): (304) 525-1001 or (800) 333-3333

Colonial Inn (Huntington): (304) 736-3466

Travelodge (Huntington): (304) 746-3451

Blenko Glass Visitor Center (Milton): (304) 743-9081

Mountaineer Opry House (Milton): (304) 743-3367

Wine Cellar Bed & Breakfast (Milton): (304) 743-5665 or (304) 743-5257

Hurricane Convention & Visitors Bureau: (304) 562-5896

Chilton House Restaurant (St. Albans): (304) 722-2918

The Wren's Nest (St. Albans): (304) 727-3224

Hamon Glass Studio (Scott Depot): (304) 757-9067

the Mound, South Charleston Convention & Visitors Bureau: (304) 746-5552 or (800) 238-9488

Sunrise Museum (Charleston): (304) 344-8035

the Brass Pineapple (Charleston): (304) 344-0748

West Virginia state capitol and capitol complex (Charleston): (304) 558-3809

governor's mansion (Charleston): (800) CALL WVA

West Virginia State Museum, Cultural Center (Charleston): (304) 558-0220 or (304) 558-0162

Mountain Stage, State Theater, Cultural Center (Charleston): (304) 558-3000 or (304) 558-0162

the shop, cultural center (Charleston): (304) 558-0220

Town Center Mall (Charleston): (304) 345-9526

Hale Street Antiques and Collectibles Mall (Charleston): (304) 345-6040

Trans Allegheny Books (Charleston): (304) 346-0551

Taylor Books (Charleston): (304) 342-1462

Charleston Convention & Visitors Bureau: (304) 344-5075 or (800) 733-5469

Tarragon Room (Charleston): (304) 353-3636

Midland Trail Scenic Highway Association (Rainelle): (304) 632-1284 or (800) 822-US60 (in West Virginia only)

Daniel Boone Park (Charleston): (304) 348-8066

Craik-Patton House (Charleston): (304) 925-5341

Cabin Creek Quilts (Malden): (304) 925-4999 or (304) 925-9499

Samuel Shrewsbury Sr. House (Old Stone House) (Belle): (304) 949-2380 or (304) 949-2398

Glen Ferris Inn: (304) 632-1111 or (800) 924-6093

Hawks Nest State Park (Ansted): (304) 658-5212 or (800) CALL WVA

Contentment (Ansted): (304) 465-5032 or (304) 658-4006

Canyon Rim Visitors Center (Lansing): (304) 574-2115

New River Gorge National River (Glen Jean): (304) 465-0508

Class VI River Runners (Lansing): (304) 574-0704 or (800) CLASS VI

the White Horse (Fayetteville): (304) 574-1400

Ridge Rider Mountain Bikes (Fayetteville): (304) 574-BIKE

New River Balloons (Fayetteville): (304) 465-8876 or (304) 574-2087

Morris Harvey House (Fayetteville): (304) 574-1179

Sedona Grill (Fayetteville): (304) 574-3411

Sarge's Dive Shop (Summersville): (304) 872-1782 or (304) 872-4048

Country Road Inn (Summersville): (304) 872-1620 or (800) 434-8852

Historic Brock House Bed and Breakfast Inn (Summersville): (304) 872-4887

Midland Trail Gallery (Lookout): (304) 438-8649

Babcock State Park (Clifftop): (304) 438-6205 or (800) CALL WVA

the Greenbrier (White Sulphur Springs): (304) 536-1110 or (800) 624-6070

4

Coal Country

Getting there: From Charleston, take I-64 west to the start of the drive on Route 52 south, just west of Huntington. This drive can also be started at the other end, on Route 52 north from Bluefield.

Highlights: Pilgrim Glass, Williamson, Matewan, the Hatfields and the McCoys, Coal Heritage Trail, Beckley, Tamarack: The Best of West Virginia, Bramwell, Bluefield. This drive is easily completed in a day or two, with overnight stays possible in the Huntington (see Chapter 1) or Bluefield areas at the start or end of the drive.

As soon as you turn off I-64 onto Route 52, you've entered rural West Virginia. This drive, through the heart of West Virginia's coal country, reveals the heart, soul, history, and culture of this unique region. It's a drive you will remember long after you've turned off the ignition.

The interesting stops begin soon after you get on Route 52. The turn for Pilgrim Glass on the left is almost immediate and you don't want to miss it if it's open.

Pilgrim Glass, located near Ceredo, is famous for producing glowing exotic colors. The mouth-blown glass products are famous worldwide and people come from everywhere to visit the factory and buy thousands of pieces annually.

Pilgrim products became famous thanks to three Italian craftsmen who made the glassware well-known in the 1950s, 1960s, and 1970s. In 1987, Cameo Glass, made popular by Emile Galle in the 1800s, had a resurgence at Pilgrim Glass. Kelsey Murphey, a talented woman who started with the company that same year, developed and produced Cameo Glass, making the antique glass of tomorrow. Today, glass collectors from around the world treasure Pilgrim's Cameo Glass designs.

More recently, Cranberry Glass has become quite popular, in that it's the most difficult of all glass colors to produce (solid gold is fused with lead crystal). Even if you don't buy a famous Pilgrim design, the tour and glassblowing are well worth the stop.

Back out on Route 52, the drive down into coal country begins. There's really not much to see for the first 65 miles or so, as you wind along the Big Sandy River and Tug Fork toward Williamson. The drive is interspersed with a few small towns, but there is very little commercial activity and few tourists pass this way. As you get close to Williamson, you'll pass through the Laurel Lake Wildlife Management Area, a 12,854-acre natural area that offers camping, hiking, swimming, and picnicking.

Williamson is a good place to stop for a rest or a meal before heading into coal country. Sports fans will enjoy the sporting atmosphere of the popular local restaurant, Starters, which is in the historic downtown shopping district.

Just down the street, at the courthouse square, be sure to stop by the Coal House. This interesting monument to the region's coal culture was built out of 65 tons of local coal.

Take Route 52 out of Williamson and then watch for the right-hand turn to Matewan after 12 miles. Be sure to allow a few hours to explore the sad events that made Matewan famous.

Situated on Tug Fork, Matewan was founded in 1897 when the Williamson Coalfield, owned by Norfolk & Western Railway, opened in the area. Matewan served as a stop on the N&W's main line and supplied goods to the surrounding mining communities. Miners, railroad workers, and locals caroused and gambled in Matewan's many saloons.

In the 1920s, Matewan was the site of a bloody confrontation between locals and mine company detectives. The United Mine Workers of America were attempting to organize area coal miners, but those who joined were fired and evicted from their homes, which were owned by the company. On May 19, 1920, Chief of Police Sid Hatfield and Mayor Cable Testerman confronted Baldwin-Felts detectives who had been hired to evict miners. Shots were fired, leaving the mayor, seven detectives, and two miners dead.

Sid Hatfield became a hero to the miners, but he was gunned down in retaliation a year later on the McDowell County Courthouse steps in Welch. Union activist Ed Chambers was also killed during the encounter. Their deaths led to many other disturbances, including the armed march of miners through the southern coalfields and a showdown at Logan County's Blair Mountain between more than 10,000 miners, the mine operators, and hundreds of federal troops.

John Sayles's 1987 feature film, *Matewan* (which was filmed in Thurmond) brought national acclaim and thousands of visitors to the town. Many important locations and buildings can still be explored today, thanks to the excellent brochure, "Matewan: A Walking Tour," which is produced by the Matewan Development Center and is available almost anywhere in town.

All along Mate Street, you'll find historic sites of interest, including the headquarters building for the Baldwin-Felts detectives; the old Matewan Cafe, once a booming saloon; the old Matewan National Bank, where the massacre started and bullet holes can still be seen; and the Hatfield Building, the present-day location of the Matewan Development Center.

Across the railroad tracks, follow the map to Warm Hollow, site of the Anderson Ferrell House, where Ellison Hatfield died on August 9, 1882, after an attack two days earlier by three McCoy brothers, sons of Randolph McCoy. Matewan and the rest of Mingo County are also famous as the location of the 1880s feud between the Hatfields and the McCoys and this is just one reminder.

Ellison's brother, Devil Anse Hatfield, executed the three McCoy brothers near Matewan. This triggered a feud that fascinated the rest of the country. Bounty hunters, including McCoy family members, made raids against the Hatfields, leading to many deaths. In 1888, the Hatfields attacked the McCoy homestead in Kentucky and killed a son and daughter and seriously wounded Randolph McCoy's wife. The killings finally stopped in the 1890s, but the legends live on.

Once back on Route 52, look for the turnoff after 10 miles to Sarah Ann and the Hatfield Family Cemetery, located on a foreboding hill. You can park and walk to the pretty spot, where you'll find Devil Hatfield's grave and monument, along with the final resting places of many other family members (note that several died on the same day).

The drive continues through pretty country, including lots of curves in the road and many dips down into small towns and hollers. In Welch, Route 52 picks up the Coal Heritage Trail (brochure available at local shops and from the helpful Southern West Virginia Convention and Visitors Bureau or the Bluestone Visitors and Convention Bureau). This road starts in Beckley on Route 16 and then meets Route 52 in Welch for the drive down to Bluefield.

The Coal Heritage Trail traverses four southern West Virginia counties in the heart of Appalachia's coalfields.

Anchored at Beckley and Bluefield, where I-77/I-64 crosses the broad plateau of Flat Top Mountain, the drive allows visitors to explore this fascinating piece of industrial history in America.

Coal—called by the ancient Greeks "the rock that burns"—powered the modernization of America. Rich coal-bearing regions like southern West Virginia were transformed in the late nineteenth century into teeming industrial civilizations.

The completion of the Chesapeake & Ohio in 1873 and the Norfolk & Western in 1883 opened up the southern West Virginia coalfields. Soon, thousands of coal miners and their families crowded into the rugged river valleys where independent coal operators boldly opened mining ventures.

West Virginia's sturdy coal miners came from all over the world. Black Americans from the Deep South joined Eastern European immigrants seeking a better life and poured into the sprawling coal camps which housed the workers.

More than 100,000 miners toiled underground in the industry's glory years, laboriously hand loading the "black diamonds" that transformed the United States from a rural nation into an international industrial power. Five billion tons of the world's finest industrial fuel flowed out along the smoothly grated roadbeds of the N&W and the C&O, hauled by the most powerful steam locomotives ever designed.

Although coal mining was dark, dirty, and dangerous work, many miners enjoyed the unique chore. Some old-timers still reminisce about the close sense of community which united the inhabitants of more than 500 small company towns that were once situated along the Coal Heritage Trail.

The road winds past company stores, miners' houses, massive railroad yards, and company towns. Visitors can experience the coal society and heritage that still exists and gain remarkable insight into a unique part of American history.

Trailheads are situated in Beckley, at the Exhibition Coal

Mine, and in Bluefield, at the Eastern Regional Coal Archives. Mile markers along the highway indicate sites of interest.

If you would like to complete the Beckley portion of the drive and then return to Route 52, you will be well rewarded. The 56-mile drive up to Beckley is quite windy and will take at least a half day for the round-trip diversion. You may want to plan a night in Beckley before returning to Route 52.

Route 16 winds along through small towns like Wolf Pen before reaching the coal town of Itmann 28 miles after Welch. It's hard to miss the huge and ornate company store, where workers bought almost everything with company script. It's in the *National Register of Historic Places* and is a large reminder of the huge role coal played in the development of this part of the state.

Route 16 continues to parallel the railroad tracks that carried the coal out from towns like Mullens, Corrine, Stephenson, Tams, Stotesbury, Sophia, and Crab Orchard. The twisting drive leads for 28 more miles into Beckley and the Exhibition Coal Mine.

Situated in New River Park, the Exhibition Coal Mine features 1,500 feet of underground passages of the mine operated by the Phillips family in the late 1800s. Visitors ride on a "man trip" car guided through the mine by veteran miners for an authentic view of low-seam coal mining, from its earliest manual stages to modernized operation. A museum features displays of coal companies in West Virginia and artifacts used during the early mining era.

Nearby, take a few steps back in time and discover what it was like to live in a company house in the coal camps of West Virginia. This restored three-room house was moved from a Sprague coal camp owned by the New River Coal Company, which was open from 1925 through the 1940s. A community of houses was built and owned by a coal company and then rented to working men and their families. Coal camps had all the necessities to function in everyday life, including a company store, company doctors, and churches.

The city of Beckley has also restored and moved a coal camp superintendent's house from Skelton to the Exhibition Coal Mine. The 88-year-old, three-story structure was built to be similar to houses from owner Samuel Dixon's home in Skelton, England. It provides another interesting example of coal camp life. The first floor re-creates the house, while the second floor includes a reproduction of the company doctor's office, a barbershop, and a company-store post office. The attic may eventually include a gallery featuring local West Virginia artists.

Beckley also serves as a great base for exploring the rest of southern West Virginia's treasures (see Chapter 5). The Southern West Virginia Convention and Visitors Bureau can serve as a great resource for planning exploration.

If you're in Beckley during the summer, contact Theatre West Virginia to see if it has a performance scheduled while you're in town. This popular amphitheater near the New River Gorge has been staging plays like *Hatfields & McCoys* and *Honey in the Rock* for more than 35 years. The stunning outdoor setting and professional presentations make the plays well worth seeing.

Beckley is also the home of Tamarack: The Best of West Virginia. This modern 59,000-square-foot West Virginia arts-and-crafts retail and visitor center showcases work and products from throughout the state. Tamarack features a juried selection of West Virginia–made crafts and agricultural products, as well as handcraft demonstrations, workshops, performances, and festivals. If you want to take home something special, be sure to visit Tamarack at the Beckley Travel Plaza at milepost 44 on I-77. Plan to spend several hours.

Back in Welch at Route 52, the Coal Heritage Trail continues its winding way down to Bluefield. Many more coal towns follow, including Elkhorn at milepost 16, an intact mining village with many company houses and small churches for the different ethnic groups who mined coal.

Serious coal historians may want to take the turnoff for Pocahontas, Virginia, near Bramwell. The Pocahontas Exhibition Mine features many artifacts and mining implements, as well as a view of the 13-foot seam of mighty Pocahontas coal, which guides say has been viewed by more than one million visitors. The mine, opened in 1882, produced more than 44 million tons of coal during its 73 years of operation.

Pocahontas coal was even more renowned for its quality than its amazing quantity. The "smokeless" purity of the coal allowed it to become the chosen fuel for the U.S. Navy. The town of Pocahontas joined with the Pocahontas Operators Association and laid out the display mine, which was the world's first such show mine. It's well worth a country road drive into Virginia (for more ideas, see *Country Roads of Virginia*).

Back in Bramwell, be sure to stop for a few hours or the night. This fascinating little town was once considered the richest town in the United States for its size, with as many as 14 millionaires living here in the early 1900s. Settled in 1885 by the largest owner of coal lands in the Pocahontas coalfield, the Flat Top Coal Land Association, Bramwell flourished with businesses, a busy train station, and an active social life. The depression in the early 1930s hurt the coal industry and the riches of Bramwell.

Today, many reminders of Bramwell's gilded past exist in the well-preserved buildings. The best way to enjoy this quiet town is to stay at one of Bramwell's fine B&Bs. One of the best bets is the Perry House, a Victorian bed-and-breakfast inn. Other possibilities include the Bluestone Inn Bed and Breakfast and Three Oaks and a Quilt Bed and Breakfast Inn.

The Perry House, with hosts Charlie and Charlotte Sacre, provides a perfect Bramwell and coal-country base. Built in 1902 for the cashier of the Bank of Bramwell, it remained in the Perry family until 1982, when the Sacres bought it and lovingly restored it into a fine B&B. The guest rooms and public areas are quite comfortable and providing an even more private retreat, there's even a three-bedroom cottage out back that was built for a coalfield doctor in 1898.

The Bramwell Millionaire Garden Club provides an excellent walking-tour map and background for Bramwell. Highlights include the 1888 town hall, the business block, the Cooper House, the Bank of Bramwell, the first office of the Pocahontas Land Company, the McGuffin House, the Mann House (and the children's playhouse across the river), the Goodwill House, and the Thomas House and garage apartment. You'll never tire of wandering the streets of Bramwell.

Route 52 leads right into Bluefield and the end of the Coal Heritage Trail. Right outside Bramwell, you'll pass Pinnacle Rock State Park on the right. This huge geological formation features a large sandstone pinnacle, with a rugged stone staircase leading to the top for a panoramic view of several counties.

Bluefield developed into a relatively large city, thanks to the coal boom. Today, there are many fascinating places to visit.

In keeping with the coal theme, the first stop should be the Eastern Regional Coal Archives, located on the second floor of the Craft Memorial Library at 600 Commerce Street. The huge collection, which is completely accessible to the public, includes more than 50,000 photos, letters, company records, books, music, tapes, film, newspapers, tools, and many other fascinating artifacts and memorabilia. Dr. Stuart McGehee is the lively archivist for this fascinating place.

The rest of Bluefield features a wide array of Victorian

architecture listed in the *National Register of Historic Places*. A walking tour is available from the Bluestone Visitors and Convention Bureau at 500 Bland Street.

This building also houses the Bluefield Area Arts and Crafts Center, which includes an art gallery with a different exhibit each month, a center shop with handmade crafts and artwork for sale, the Summit Theatre, the Science Center of West Virginia (great for kids), and David's Restaurant—a tasty way to end this drive.

In the Area

Pilgrim Glass (Ceredo): (304) 453-3553

Laurel Lake Wildlife Management Area (Lenore): (304) 475-2823

Starters (Williamson): (304) 235-8600

the Coal House (Williamson): (304) 235-5240

Matewan Development Center: (304) 426-4239

Southern West Virginia Convention and Visitors Bureau (Beckley): (304) 252-2244 or (800) VISIT WV

Exhibition Coal Mine (Beckley): (304) 256-1747

Theatre West Virginia (Beckley): (304) 256-6800 or (800) 666-9142

Tamarack: The Best of West Virginia (Beckley): (304) 256-6843 or (800) TAMARACK

Pocahontas Exhibition Mine (Pocahontas, Virginia): (540) 945-2134

Perry House (Bramwell): (304) 248-8145

Bluestone Inn Bed and Breakfast (Bramwell): (304) 248-8337

Three Oaks and a Quilt Bed and Breakfast Inn (Bramwell): (304) 248-8316

Bramwell Millionaire Garden Club: (304) 248-7114, (304) 248-7202, or (304) 248-7252

Pinnacle Rock State Park (Bramwell): (800) CALL WVA

Bluestone Visitors and Convention Bureau (Bluefield): (304) 325-8438

Bluefield Area Arts and Crafts Center: (304) 325-8000

the Summit Theatre (Bluefield): (304) 325-8000

Science Center of West Virginia (Bluefield): (304) 325-8855

David's Restaurant (Bluefield): (304) 325-9291

5

Southern West Virginia

Getting there: From Charleston, take I-77 south to the start of the drive on Route 20 north, just east of Bluefield. This drive can also be started at the other end, on Route 20 at I-64 near Sandstone.

Highlights: Pipestem State Park, Bluestone Lake, Bluestone State Park, Hinton, Pence Springs Hotel, Sandstone Falls. This drive is easily completed in a day or two, with overnight stays possible in the Bluefield area (see Chapter 4) at the start or end of the drive or at Pipestem State Park or the Pence Springs Hotel.

The road down to Route 20 is speedy on I-77, but it belies what is to come. If you're heading down to this part of West Virginia in the winter, you may want to plan some skiing at Winterplace Ski Resort, the state's southernmost spot for skiing. It's located just off I-77, near Flat Top.

Just 15 miles farther south, you'll find Route 20. As soon as you turn off I-77 onto Route 20, you immediately slow down, thanks to the winding roads and scenic countryside. This drive through the heart of southern West Virginia may be short, but it's not lacking in things to see and do along the way. If you want lots of information in advance, contact the helpful Southern West Virginia Convention and Visitors Bureau.

The interesting scenery begins soon after you get on Route 20. The road climbs into the mountains, passing through small towns like Athens and Lerona before reaching the entrance to Pipestem State Park after about 15 minutes.

A windswept plateau provides the setting for this park's array of accommodations and recreational facilities. The unique name for the resort was taken from the native pipestem bush. The bush's hollow woody stems were used by nine different Indian tribes in the making of pipes. Whether you're stopping by for a quick visit or a few days, this is another great West Virginia state park.

Resting on the lip of the Bluestone River Gorge, Pipestem's main lodge features rooms and dining, as well as a commanding view of the gorge and the impressive mountain ranges of the park's rugged locale. Another completely different accommodation option, Mountain Creek Lodge, provides a remote hideaway at the base of the 1,000-foot Bluestone canyon (accessible only by aerial tramway). There are also 25 fully equipped cottages and an 82-site campground.

The beautiful surroundings of Pipestem are laced with miles of hiking and bridle trails, scenic overlooks, and many recreational opportunities. Among the abundant outdoor sports, the most popular include horseback riding, tennis, golf, fishing, hiking, boating, swimming, and cross-country skiing. Year-round nature programs are also offered, as well as performances in the outdoor amphitheater and arts and crafts in the shop.

Just outside the park entrance, about a half-mile farther up Route 20, be sure to plan a meal at the Oak Supper Club. This unique restaurant, with its signature 800-year-old giant oak tree, is an ideal Route 20 dining respite, whether you're staying at Pipestem or just driving through.

Owner Jim Bolinger and chef Larry Merrill Jr. have made the Oak Supper Club a tasty Route 20 stop for more than 20 years. The rustic and casual atmosphere provides the perfect setting for carefully prepared fresh food. Some of the menu possibilities include the club's signature barbecue, duckling, fresh rainbow trout, prime rib, and something truly different called the Horseshoe Platter (an open-faced sandwich platter, topped with a spicy cheese sauce and french fries).

Back on Route 20, long and narrow Bluestone Lake comes into view and the road runs parallel to it for several miles. There are several excellent places to pull off for views and pictures.

Bluestone Lake is the state's third largest, comprising 2,100 surface acres. Boating, fishing, and hunting are quite popular at the lake and the adjacent wildlife management area. Bordering the lake, Bluestone State Park features cabins, camping, boats, fishing, and hiking.

Completed in 1952, the Bluestone Dam, which Route 20 crosses, tames the joining waters of the New and Bluestone Rivers to form the lake. There's an interpretive center at the dam.

The next stop is Hinton, one of West Virginia's most interesting towns. Hinton marks the confluence of the New River Gorge National River, the Bluestone National Scenic River, and the Greenbrier River, making it an historically important transportation town.

Hinton became a thriving city with the advent of coal mining and railroad construction in the 1870s. The history of Hinton cannot be separated from the history of coal and the C&O Railway, which made the town a major C&O terminal yard.

In 1873, there were only six families in Hinton. The town then experienced a building boom, which began with the Tomkies Building on Third Avenue in 1895 and ended with the

Big Four building in 1907, with many large and interesting structures being built during the intervening years. By 1907, the population had increased to more than 6,000.

Most of the downtown commercial and residential buildings have survived demolition or major alterations. In 1984, the downtown Hinton historic district was placed in the *National Register of Historic Places*. A walk through Hinton is like a walk through early West Virginia history.

The architecture of the district reflects the eclecticism of the Victorian era and the various tastes of owners and builders. Styles include Victorian, classical revival, high Victorian, American Four Square, Second Empire, and much more. Church styles include American Gothic, classical, and Greek revival.

There are dozens of highlights on the walking tour (get a map from the Summers County Visitor Center or many other places in town). Some buildings not to be missed include Tomkies Department Store, the Big Four building (a lodge for four brotherhoods), the CB Mahon General Store, the Parker Opera House, the C&O commissary, the James Row Apartments, the First United Methodist Church, Summers County Courthouse, McCreery Hotel, the C&O passenger depot, and the National Bank of Summers. This is a town for walking.

If you're not staying at the Pence Springs Hotel, Hinton provides an ideal overnight stop. Two friendly and comfortable B&Bs right in the historic district that are highly recommended are Historic Hinton Manor and Heritage House Bed & Breakfast. Dining spots in the historic district include Kirk's and the Bobcat's Den.

Route 3 intersects with Route 20 in Hinton, providing an easy diversion farther into southern West Virginia. Your goal is the Pence Springs Hotel, just 15 minutes from Hinton.

Route 3 follows the quiet Greenbrier River and the (usually) quiet railroad tracks, but the area wasn't quite so quiet when the legendary John Henry helped build the C&O Railroad's Big Bend Tunnel just outside Hinton. There's a monument alongside the road in honor of this powerful steel-driving man.

A few miles farther, in Lowell, look for the Graham House on the left. This large log home built in the 1770s was the home of an early settler, Col. James Graham. While showing what frontier life was like, the house tour also depicts an Indian attack in 1777, which resulted in the deaths of Graham's son and a family friend. Graham's daughter was abducted and he did not gain her return until 1785. Legend has it that Graham reversed the shoes on his horses so the Indians wouldn't follow them home.

You'll know the diversionary drive to Pence Springs was worth it as soon as you pull up to the Pence Springs Hotel.

Formerly know as the Grand Hotel, the Pence Springs Hotel is one of the historic old mineral spas of an early time in the Virginias. Opened in 1918, it was a premier resort in the Roaring Twenties, when more than 10 trains arrived daily, bringing guests lured by the award-winning mineral water and the peaceful countryside. But the Great Depression forced the closure of the Grand Hotel and it operated as a girl's school and a dude ranch before being purchased by the state and operated as the state prison for women from 1947 to 1983. Ashby Berkley, a local businessman, bought the old hotel in 1987 and has lovingly restored it. Now guests love visiting the Pence Springs Hotel.

The again-popular hotel offers 26 rooms, traditional cooking in the dining room or on the sun porch, and a popular basement pub. Several of the prison rooms have been left in their original state. Just down the hill, the old spring still spouts the famous water for present-day visitors to enjoy. The famed Pence Springs Flea Market, near the hotel, is West Virginia's largest Sunday market, with everything from antiques to local produce.

Pence Springs is one of a number of historic springs and

resorts in the area. Of course, White Sulphur Springs and the Greenbrier are the most famous spots (see Chapter 3), but many other towns in the counties of Monroe, Summers, and Greenbrier feature remnants of the earlier era when springs resorts were so popular. The Monroe County Historical Society has prepared a brochure called "The Springs Trail," which provides details about many of the towns in the area. It's available from the Lewisburg Visitors Bureau. The trail includes parts of Routes 12, 3, 60, and 122.

Visitors once came by the thousands to where the healing waters flowed and many grand resorts flourished. Some of the sites along the route near Hinon include Salt Sulphur Springs and the Indian Creek covered bridge (see Chapter 6), Red Sulphur Springs (except for the spring, not a trace remains of this large resort), and Blue Sulphur Springs (only the spring pavilion remains of this popular nineteenth-century property).

Back on Route 20 in Hinton, the drive continues north, following the New River and the ever-present train tracks. Just three miles before the intersection with I-64 and the end of the drive, be sure to stop at the Sandstone Falls overlook. The river-wide falls drop an average of 10 feet, marking the upper extent of navigation in the river's northern stretch.

This pretty spot is like an overview of the entire area. It takes any country road driver's love of West Virginia to new heights.

In the Area

Winterplace Ski Resort (Flat Top): (304) 787-3221 or (800) 607-7669

Southern West Virginia Convention and Visitors Bureau (Beckley): (304) 252-2244 or (800) VISIT WV

Pipestem State Park: (304) 466-1800 or (800) CALL WVA

the Oak Supper Club (Pipestem): (304) 466-4800

Bluestone Lake (Hinton): (304) 466-1234

Bluestone State Park (Hinton): (304) 466-1922 or (800) CALL
  WVA

Hinton historic district: (304) 466-5420

Summers County Visitor Center (Hinton): (304) 466-5420

Historic Hinton Manor (Hinton): (304) 466-3930

Heritage House Bed & Breakfast (Hinton): (304) 466-6070

Kirk's (Hinton): (304) 466-4600

Bobcat's Den (Hinton): (304) 466-3550

Graham House (Lowell): (304) 466-5502 or (304) 466-3321

Pence Springs Hotel: (304) 445-2606 or (800) 826-1829

Pence Springs Flea Market: (304) 445-2606

Lewisburg Visitors Bureau: (304) 645-1000 or (800) 833-2068

Riverside Inn (Pence Springs): (304) 445-7469 or (800) 826-
  1829

6

The Potomac Highlands

Getting there: From Charleston, take I-77 south to Route 460 west and the start of the drive on Route 219 north, just across the Virginia state line. This drive can also be started at the other end, at the intersection of Route 219 and Route 250 in Huttonsville.

Highlights: Organ Cave, Lewisburg, Lost World Caverns, Hillsboro, Elk River Touring Center, Snowshoe Mountain Resort. This drive is easily completed in a long weekend, with stops along the way in Lewisburg or the Snowshoe Mountain area.

This drive, crossing right through the middle of some of West Virginia's prettiest scenery, actually starts in Virginia. But you're only in the Old Dominion (see *Country Roads of Virginia*) for a brief period of time before you head back into the hills of West Virginia.

Route 219 begins its curvy ascent through the state with a few small towns and the pretty scenery that just hints at the natural attractions ahead. About 17 miles into the drive, look for the Indian Creek covered bridge on the right, near the Route 122 intersection. Though no longer in use, it has been restored to its original condition.

About 10 more miles up the road, the quiet town of Union

is well worth a stop and stretch. Union is the county seat and the Monroe County Historical Society Museum on Main Street can provide an interesting walking-tour map for exploring the town's architecture and history. Highlights include the courthouse and jail, the cemetery, the Watchman Office and Print Shop, and the Old Rehoboth Church (two miles east of town).

Back on Route 219, head into Ronceverte and look for the right-hand turn on Route 63 to Organ Cave.

Pioneers have explored Organ Cave since 1704. Thomas Jefferson visited it in 1791, and according to legend, discovered the remains of a prehistoric dinosaur now displayed in Philadelphia. Organ Cave was a vital source of saltpeter during the Civil War, which was used for making gunpowder. Wooden hoppers were used to leach the saltpeter from cave soil, and 37 of them can still be seen today. Robert E. Lee held religious services for more than 1,100 men in Organ Cave's huge entrance room.

Today's explorers will discover much history and beauty in Organ Cave. It is one of the longest known cave systems in the United States, with more than 40 miles of mapped passageways. Teams of experienced cavers continue exploration of new passages.

Organ Cave was opened commercially in 1835 and has been welcoming visitors to its cool 55-degree environment ever since. Cavern tours are unaffected by weather and the pathways are well lit for the guided tours. The highlight of a tour is the huge Church Organ, the organlike calcite formation that gave the cave its name more than a century ago.

Route 219 heads steeply down into the town of Lewisburg, where the road intersects with Route 60 (see Chapter 3). You should plan on a few hours or days in this delightful Greenbrier Valley town.

Originally called Camp Union and Fort Savannah, the town was renamed Lewisburg to honor the pioneering Lewis family. In 1774, Gen. Andrew Lewis assembled a frontier militia and led it to Point Pleasant to defeat the Shawnee in an epic battle with Chief Cornstalk. Chartered in 1782 by the Virginia assembly, the frontier town prospered as a way station on the James River and Kanawha Turnpike.

Lewisburg was a Southern outpost for most of the Civil War, but the battle of Lewisburg, fought on May 23, 1862, was won by Union forces under George Crook (who later caught Geronimo).

Thanks to an unusual collection of eighteenth- and nineteenth-century buildings, a large part of town is designated a National Register Historic District. The Lewisburg Visitors Center at 105 Church Street provides an excellent walking-tour guide of the town, as well as many other useful pamphlets. Highlights include Carnegie Hall, the Old Stone Church, North House, the Greenbrier County Library, Andrew Lewis Park (Lewis Springs), the Greenbrier County Courthouse, the Confederate Cemetery, and the former Greenbrier Military School.

Another of the town's highlights is the General Lewis Inn, where you can stop for a quick visit, a meal, or the night. The east wing of this historic inn was originally the 1834 house of John Withrow. The lobby and west wing were added in 1928. The entire establishment is furnished with locally collected antiques and every bed is at least 100 years old. The inn's founder, Randolph K. Hock, and his wife, Mary Milton Noel, collected all these beautiful pieces for their guests' enjoyment.

Guests check in at the front desk, a hand-built 1760 walnut-and-pine masterpiece that welcomed Patrick Henry and Thomas Jefferson when it was used at the old Sweet Chalybeate Springs Hotel nearby. Memory Hall is packed with memorabilia from earlier times in Greenbrier County.

All the guest rooms are unique and allow a chance to fall

asleep amidst history. If you're hungry, the dining room provides old-fashioned cooking. Specialties include fried chicken, mountain trout, country ham, grilled pork chops, and steak, accompanied by hot homemade breads and desserts.

Other accommodation options in Lewisburg include Lynn's Inn B&B, Minnie Manor B&B, or the Budget Host Fort Savannah Inn. Dining options are plentiful and include the General Lewis Inn, the Fort Savannah Inn, Food & Friends, and several others.

If you're into antiques and other shopping, Lewisburg is a gold mine. Old general store fans will love the Old General Store on Washington Street. It is filled with old-fashioned favorites and handmade gifts, including homemade peanut butter, comb honey, maple syrup, buckwheat flour, bulk spices, and much more.

Lewisburg is also an ideal base for exploring the surrounding countryside. The mountains and the Greenbrier River provide many outdoor pleasures and several companies can help you enjoy Mother Nature, West Virginia style.

Mountain bikes are big business throughout the state and there are two excellent companies to help you enjoy the mountains and the Greenbrier River Trail. Free Spirit Adventures and High Country Bikes both offer rentals, guided tours and trips, and many other services.

The Greenbrier River Trail is an extraordinary natural resource which no Greenbrier River Valley visitor should miss. The trail was wonderfully converted from an old C&O Railroad bed that once paralleled the Greenbrier River. Today, the level 76-mile trail hosts bikers and hikers instead of trains. The trail starts just outside Lewisburg, near Caldwell, so Lewisburg is an ideal base for the southern end of the trail (outfitters can help), while Marlinton is a popular stopover midway (milepost 56) along the trail.

The Greenbrier River is also a popular recreational asset. If you would like to canoe part of the peaceful river, contact the Greenbrier River Company in nearby Ronceverte, which can help with paddling and accommodation packages, multi-day trips, rentals, shuttles, fishing, biking, and much more. The company also has an excellent campground right on the banks of the river.

Lewisburg is also the base for exploring Lost World Caverns, just outside town on Fairview Road. These popular caverns were discovered by Virginia Polytechnic Institute cavers in 1942, when they descended to the cave's floor through a grapevine-covered opening. The spot was known as Grapevine Cave, until it was renamed Lost World Caverns, renovated, and opened to the public in 1981.

The formations and caves in Lost World Caverns are big enough to get lost in, but the tour guide will keep you in the correct place. Some of the highlights include the Snow Chandelier, Goliath, and Ice Cream Wall. Along with the regular walking tour, unique wild cave adventures are also available.

Back on Route 219, the exploration continues. Route 219 runs roughly parallel with the Greenbrier River (and many trail access points) and through rolling farmland. Pocahontas County is at the heart of the Potomac highlands.

About 25 miles north of Lewisburg, you reach the entrance for Beartown State Park. This interesting park features a boardwalk that leads through a wild array of sandstone rock formations and quiet forests. It's a peaceful diversion from driving.

Just a mile up the road, look for the turnoff to Droop Mountain Battlefield State Park. This now-peaceful park was the site of a bloody Civil War battle that claimed more than 400 lives. Confederate troops were driven out of West Virginia for good after this battle, fought on November 6, 1863. Highlights include a museum, hiking trails, and trenches. If you would like to spend the night in this historic and beautiful area, contact the Yew Mountain Lodge, a convenient and tranquil 500-acre retreat.

Route 219 leads immediately into Hillsboro and another interesting Greenbrier Valley town. Hillsboro is best known as the birthplace of Pearl S. Buck, one of America's most distinguished writers. Fans come from afar to visit the restored home where Pearl was born, which is a far cry from the home where she lived in China for 40 years.

Located right on Route 219, the house was built by the Stulting family (Pearl's grandparents), who had emigrated to America from Holland in 1847. On June 26, 1892, Pearl Comfort Sydenstricker was born. Her missionary parents, having lost earlier children in China, had returned to the United States for a few months for Pearl's birth.

Writing under her married name of Pearl S. Buck, she won the hearts of Americans with her famous novel, *The Good Earth*, for which she won the Pulitzer Prize for literature in 1932. For the high quality of her literary work, Pearl won the Nobel Prize in Literature in 1938. She is the only American woman to receive both awards.

The restored house is a white-columned beauty, with furnishings and artifacts from the period, as well as many articles from Pearl's life. A gift shop sells autographed books, first-day covers of Pearl S. Buck stamps, and many additional souvenirs.

The Pearl S. Buck Museum complex also includes the Sydenstricker House, which was the birthplace of Pearl's father. This pretty farmhouse was dismantled and transported 40 miles to its present location.

The rest of Hillsboro provides for a restful stop. One of the most popular rest stops is the Hillsboro General Store on Route 219. Established in 1893, this classic general store features everything from antiques to country ham. It's a true step back in time.

For more shopping on Route 219, head to Morning Star Folk Arts. Dwight and Elaine Diller feature a wide array of West Virginia Heritage Dolls, nineteenth-century traditional music performed by Dwight on banjo, fiddle, and guitar, and the work of many local artists and crafters. The Four Winds Cafe nearby provides filling meals in an airy and old-fashioned atmosphere.

If you would like to stay in the Hillsboro area, call Leslee McMarty at the Current to see if she has a room. The pretty 1905 farmhouse, located near the banks of the Greenbrier River, has four spacious rooms, a large deck, and delicious country breakfasts.

Just up the road on Route 219, look for the Route 39/55 turnoff to the left at Mill Point. This diversion is worth the extra hour or so of driving.

Route 39/55 leads into the pretty Cranberry Mountain area and to one of West Virginia's special roads, the Highland Scenic Highway. This beautiful National Forest Scenic Byway, right through the heart of the Monongahela National Forest, extends 43 miles from Richwood back to Route 219, seven miles south of Marlinton (this makes for a nice loop back to Route 219). The highway follows Route 39/55 for 21 miles from Richwood to the Cranberry Mountain Visitor Center and then turns onto State Route 150 for the 22-mile parkway section.

If you have time and you've timed it right, you may want to head into Richwood for a uniquely West Virginia experience. Richwood, known as the ramp capital of the world, is home to a huge festival in April that celebrates ramps, a version of wild leeks that have a unique taste and odor. You have to see them to believe them and you can see them by contacting the Richwood Area Chamber of Commerce.

The highway traverses the mountainous terrain of the Allegheny highlands and plateau, rising from 2,325 feet in

Richwood to more than 4,500 feet on the parkway. Four scenic overlooks located on the parkway portion provide for spectacular views of the surrounding ridges and valleys. Spring blossoms, summer wildflowers, and autumn leaves offer color throughout the seasons.

The Cranberry Glades Botanical Area features the largest area of bogs in the state. Typical of acidic wetlands found in Canada, a half-mile boardwalk allows exploration of this fragile area. The Falls of Hills Creek Scenic Area features three waterfalls that cascade over rock layers of sandstone and shale. The three-quarter-mile trail provides access to the falls.

More than 150 miles of trails can be found along the highway. Three campgrounds are located just a short drive off the route, while the Cranberry Mountain Lodge provides a perfect and private mountain retreat. It's an ideal (and typical) West Virginia country road diversion.

Route 219 leads into Marlinton and a few town attractions. Right before heading into town, be sure to stop at the Pocahontas County Historical Museum on the right. Located in an old 1904 frame house, the museum features the history of the county from Indian days to the present. Other highlights include the Pearl S. Buck Library, a log cabin, and a local cemetery.

Marlinton is a perfect base for exploring the Greenbrier River Trail, Watoga State Park, and the rest of Pocahontas County. With a wide variety of typical state park activities and amenities, Watoga State Park is a great place to spend the day or night. Cabins are available at the park and Marlinton offers several excellent B&B options, including the Old Clark Inn and Das Gasthaus.

The next stop in this Potomac highlands wonderland is Slatyfork. Thanks to the rugged mountains and several successful resorts, the Slatyfork area is a vibrant outdoor community.

To get a sense of this community, stop by Sharp's Country Store on Route 219. For more than 100 years, the Sharp family has operated a mercantile business in Slatyfork. The present store opened in 1927 and is pretty much like it was back then, with dark oak shelves heavily laden with food-stuffs, beverages, supplies, clothing, antiques, and collectibles. There are numerous displays from periods of the store's history. Linda (granddaughter of founder L. D. Sharp) and her husband, Benny Eduardo, will be happy to share the store and stories.

Country road drivers will appreciate the opportunity to let someone else do the driving at the Cass Scenic Railroad State Park. A part of West Virginia's excellent state park system, this unique park offers an excursion that transports passengers back to a time when steam-driven locomotives were part of everyday life. Cass is reached by taking the new 11-mile connector road, Route 66, that runs from Slatyfork and Route 219.

The town of Cass remains relatively unchanged, with restored buildings and the charm of an old railroad town. From the country store and museum to the railroad station, you'll find plenty to do before your departure.

The Cass Scenic Railroad is the same line built in 1902 and used to haul lumber to the mill in Cass. The locomotives are also the same ones used then, while the passenger cars are old logging flatcars that have been converted into coaches.

A 90-ton locomotive, complete with thick smoke, pulls away from the station, passing the old water tower where the locomotive's tanks are filled. The train heads up the curve at Leatherback Creek and passes the Cass Shop, where the trains are serviced and repaired and where there is lots of old equipment. The train heads at full steam up two huge switchbacks and into the mountains at an amazing 11-percent grade. It stops at Whittaker Station, where you can enjoy spectacular

A steam-driven locomotive makes its way through the Cass Scenic Railroad State Park, Cass.

views and a picnic lunch. You can also continue on to Bald Knob, the second highest point in the state. The round-trip excursion to Whittaker Station takes one and one-half hours, while the exciting Bald Knob trip takes four and a half hours.

You can also stay right in Cass. The state park features beautiful six-, eight-, and 10-person cottages. The Shay Inn, located in what was the park superintendent's house, features B&B-style accommodations, country antiques, and homestyle food.

Back in Slatyfork, look for the Elk River Touring Center on the left-hand side of Route 219. This outdoor mecca is a great source for exploring the Potomac highlands by many means of transportation. Begun as a cross-country skiing center, Elk River has grown into a complete ski and mountain-biking outdoor vacation center.

Gil and Mary Willis offer accommodations in a farmhouse and a nearby cabin. They also offer some of the area's most creative dining. Their Nordic center features guided backcountry tours, lessons, a nearby lit beginner's loop, and much more for the cross-country skiing and snowshoeing enthusiast. It's a perfect spot to try this snow sport or to enjoy some serious West Virginia wilderness in the winter.

For two-wheel travelers, Elk River's mountain-biking programs are popular and extensive. Elk River offers a wide variety of daily and multi-day tours, including accommodations, meals, rentals, instruction, and more. There are also many other mountain-biking programs available at this amazing establishment.

Just up the road, look for the right-hand turn to Snowshoe Mountain Resort. This four-season resort has developed into one of West Virginia's biggest tourism draws. With some of the region's best skiing in the winter and plenty of off-season golf, mountain-biking, and hiking opportunities, Snowshoe Mountain Resort is perfect for a stay of several days. Thanks to new owner Intrawest, more than $60 million of improvements have made Snowshoe better than ever.

Snowshoe's mountaintop location, more than 180 inches of snow annually, and a wide variety of services and amenities make the resort a favorite mid-Atlantic skiing destination. A wide range of accommodations (hotels to houses), varied dining, and many après-ski possibilities add to the enjoyment. From spring to fall, Snowshoe switches from skiing to golf, mountain biking, and hiking. The award-winning Gary Player course and lots of trails, have made Snowshoe a popular spot for hackers, bikers, and hikers.

Make plans for at least one memorable meal at the Red Fox, one of the best restaurants in the state. Brian Ball and

Margaret Ann Smith welcome Snowshoe Mountain Resort visitors to this haven for fine food and atmosphere. A typical meal might include *Woodland Cobbler*, *Roast Highland Quail*, *Forester's Partridge*, *White Rock Hen*, *Mountain Trout*, *Rack of Venison*, or *Cassoulet of Field and Fowl*. It's a meal you will not soon forget.

Back down on Route 219, the road continues along the edge of the Monongahela National Forest, past the tiny towns of Mace, Mingo, and Elkwater to the drive's end at Huttonsville. This is a great place to continue along Route 250 for more West Virginia country road adventures (see Chapter 2).

In the Area

Monroe County Historical Society Museum (Union): (304) 772-5317

Organ Cave (Ronceverte): (304) 647-5551 or (800) 258-CAVE

Lewisburg Visitors Center: (304) 645-1000 or (800) 833-2068

the General Lewis Inn (Lewisburg): (304) 645-2600 or (800) 628-4454

Lynn's Inn B&B (Lewisburg): (304) 645-2003

Minnie Manor B&B (Lewisburg): (304) 647-4096

Budget Host Fort Savannah Inn (Lewisburg): (304) 645-3055 or (800) 678-3055

Food & Friends (Lewisburg): (304) 645-4548

Old General Store (Lewisburg): (304) 647-3950

Free Spirit Adventures (Lewisburg): (800) 877-4749

High Country Bikes (Lewisburg): (304) 645-5200

Greenbrier River Trail, Watoga State Park (Marlinton): (304) 799-4087 or (800) CALL WVA

Greenbrier River Company (Ronceverte): (304) 645-2760 or (800) 775-2203

Lost World Caverns (Lewisburg): (304) 645-6677

Pocahontas County Tourism Commission (Marlinton): (304) (800) 336-7009

Beartown State Park (Hillsboro): (304) 653-4254 or (800) CALL WVA

Droop Mountain Battlefield State Park (Hillsboro): (304) 653-4254 or (800) CALL WVA

Yew Mountain Lodge (Hillsboro): (304) 653-4821

Pearl S. Buck Museum (Hillsboro): (304) 653-4430

Hillsboro General Store: (304) 653-4414

Morning Star Folk Arts (Hillsboro): (304) 653-4397

Four Winds Cafe (Hillsboro): (304) 653-4335

the Current (Hillsboro): (304) 653-4722

Highland Scenic Highway (Richwood): (304) 846-2695 or (800) CALL WVA

Cranberry Mountain Visitor Center (Richwood): (304) 653-4826

Richwood Area Chamber of Commerce: (304) 846-6790

Cranberry Mountain Lodge (Richwood): (304) 242-6070

Pocahontas County Historical Museum (Marlinton): (800) 336-7009

Watoga State Park (Marlinton): (304) 799-4087 or (800) CALL WVA the Old Clark Inn (Marlinton): (304) 799-6377

Das Gasthaus (Marlinton): (304) 799-6711

Sharp's Country Store (Slatyfork): (304) 572-3547

Cass Scenic Railroad State Park: (304) 456-4300 or (800) CALL
   WVA

Shay Inn (Cass): (304) 456-4652

Elk River Touring Center (Slatyfork): (304) 572-3771

Snowshoe Mountain Resort: (304) 572-1000

the Red Fox (Snowshoe): (304) 572-1111

7

Canaan Valley and More

Getting there: From Charleston, take I-79 north and Route 33 east to the middle of the drive in Harman. You can then proceed to the start of the drive at the Virginia border on Route 33 or to the other end, Blackwater Falls State Park. This drive is easily combined with explorations of Route 219 (Chapter 6) or Route 250 (Chapter 2).

Highlights: Monongahela National Forest, Spruce Knob, Seneca Caverns, Seneca Rocks, Dolly Sods Recreation Area, Canaan Valley State Park and Conference Center, Davis, Blackwater Falls State Park. This drive is easily completed in two or three days, with an overnight stay along the way, for example, in Canaan Valley, or in Davis or Blackwater Falls State Park at the start or end of the drive.

The northern section of the Potomac highlands is West Virginia at its wildest. From the highest point in the state to some of prettiest countryside in the United States, the area in and around Canaan Valley makes for some incredible outdoor adventures.

The drive starts quietly enough in the Brandywine area, but builds to a thundering crescendo at Blackwater Falls. This is a drive in which you should take long stops to enjoy all

Mother Nature and West Virginia have to
offer once you get out of your car.

The Brandywine Recreation Area near
the Virginia border makes for an ideal
stop for hiking, camping, or swimming
at the small beach and lake. The 3.6-mile
Sawmill Trail provides a perfect leg-stretching hike. Part of the
George Washington National Forest, the area is just a prelude
to the outdoor wonders farther into the state.

Route 33 heads west into the small town of Brandywine.
Try to save a big hunger for a meal at Fat Boy's Pork Palace.
This classic West Virginia roadside restaurant, owned and run
by Mike and Sharon Burkett, features some of the South's
best pork barbecue.

After you've eaten your fill of serious barbecue, you head
up into some serious mountains. If you've run out of driving
time for the day, head for the quiet valley town of Franklin.
The Candlelight Inn on Main Street and innkeepers Carey
and Claudia Evick provide a perfect place to spend the night.
This 1910 Victorian home features three pretty guest rooms,
a hot tub and indoor pool, and a full breakfast in the morning.

Though Franklin and the Candlelight Inn can provide a
nice respite, the curvy driving continues as you head farther
into the rugged mountain landscape. There are several great
views of Germany Valley at well-marked turnoffs along the
way.

Shortly after leaving Franklin, you enter the Monongahela
National Forest. This huge woodland area encompasses more
than 901,000 acres of scenic mountains and forests. Some of
the state's best fishing, hunting, and hiking can be found in
this national forest. Much of this area is also explored in
Chapter 2.

The road makes a sharp right turn at Judy Gap, the starting point for many excursions into the Spruce Knob area.
These mountains will take you to new West Virginia heights.

Spruce Knob, at 4,860 feet, is the highest point in the state. It is easily reached by following Route 33 out of Judy Gap and then following the signs for 10 miles or so to Spruce Knob Lake and on up to the peak.

Once at the top, visitors are rewarded with stunning 360-degree rooftop views of the rough landscape. Hiking in the area, including an interpretive trail highlighting the unique windblown area, is excellent.

Back on Route 33, the natural wonders don't stop. Near Riverton, look for the turn to Seneca Caverns and descend into another West Virginia world.

West Virginia's largest caverns, Seneca Caverns are 2,500 feet above sea level, 165 feet below the surface at the deepest point, and 25 feet below the surface at the shallowest point. As you walk the three-quarter-mile passage through the caverns, you'll hear water dripping and intermittent streams flowing, which indicate that additional formations are still being created. This new growth is taking place adjacent to formations estimated to be 300 million years old.

The guided tour takes about 35 minutes and passes along well-lit level walkways. The cavern temperature is constantly 54 degrees, so you may want to bring along a sweater.

Seneca Caverns contains an abundance of snow-white and creamy-white streaks of flowstone, where water flowing in a very thin sheet over rocks has deposited mineral matter. Streaks of flowstone lace themselves with tawny colors as they drape the walls and fall over precipitous edges. In several rooms, you'll find flecks of calcite crystals woven into the flowstone, causing reflected light to dance and sparkle. This type of flowstone is called *travertine*.

The monumental cones that rise from the floor are called *stalagmites*. They are deposits of calcium carbonate that are formed by the drip of calcareous water. The formations resembling icicles hanging from the roof or side of the cavern are called *stalactites* and are also formed from the slow drip of calcareous water. To wipe the moisture from either tip would be wiping away almost 100 years of mineral deposits.

The guided tour includes Mirror Lake (an underground pool that reflects overhead formations), the Grand Ballroom (a huge room 60 feet long, 30 feet wide, and up to 70 feet high), Niagara Falls Frozen Over, and the Capitol Dome. The gentle lighting enhances the formations. Unlike many caverns in the region, Seneca Caverns isn't too commercialized or developed. It's well worth a visit.

Back on Route 33, the winding road leads down to Seneca Rocks. You'll see the rock formations rising out of the earth on your right. They draw visitors like magnets and with so much to see and do, you should plan on staying awhile.

Seneca Rocks towers almost completely vertical 900 feet above the North Fork River. The sheer rock face is broken up by a notch in the middle of the formation. This area once held a 30-foot pinnacle called the Gendarme, which toppled down in 1987.

The rock formations occurred more than 400 million years ago, when deeper rocks pushed these hard rock cliffs to the surface. You can learn much more about the formations at the Seneca Rocks Visitor Center, situated in the shadow of the rocks. The unusual nature and hardness of the rocks have made them a huge draw for rock climbers and other curious visitors.

Rock climbing is big business here in that serious climbers come from around the world to scale Seneca Rocks. Two major guide services, Seneca Rocks Climbing School and Seneca Rocks Mountain Guides, support the climbers and also hold a wide variety of classes and guided trips. If you want to try rock climbing, this is a great place to start.

Seneca Rocks Climbing School has been in the same location since 1971 and was the first guide service in the country to be accredited by the American Mountain Guides Association. Class offerings are typical of what's available in the area, with a basic weekend course, a comprehensive three-day basic course, intermediate rock skills, and leading courses. Along with courses and private guiding, Seneca Rocks Climbing School also features a full-service shop, the Gendarme, where congenial climbers have gathered for years.

Those who don't want to go vertical but still want to take in the view can take the 1.5-mile West Side Trail up to the top. It's a bit steep in spots, but well worth the hike. There's a viewing platform with one of the best views in the state.

Back down at the foot of Seneca Rocks, there's a burgeoning tourist operation. Harper's Old Country Store is at the center of it all and has been since 1902. One of the oldest continuously operated businesses in the state, this general store has served generations and is still operated by the Harper family.

The interior of the store is much the same as in 1902, with many original features and antiques. The original board floor (which must be oiled frequently), the metal-blocked ceiling, and the original shelves and counters give the visitor a feeling of stepping back in time. Along with standard merchandise, there are many West Virginia products and even a huge mounted black bear that was shot nearby. The architecture of the building, including a large front porch, represents a typical commercial establishment of the late 1800s and early 1900s.

Upstairs, the Front Porch Restaurant provides climbers, hikers, and other hungry visitors with filling food and great views of Seneca Rocks. Its fresh dough pizza is a popular choice with the climbing set.

For a short diversion before heading farther on Route 33, cavern cravers should head a few miles northeast on Route 55 to Smoke Hole Caverns. Though much more commercialized than Seneca Caverns, the actual caverns and formations are equally interesting. Some of the highlights of the guided tour include Crystal Cave Coral Pool, Rainbow Falls, and the Room of a Million Stalactites.

If you decide to stay in the area for a day or two, you have several accommodation options. Climbers generally rough it at Seneca Shadows Campground, which is a modern National Forest Service campground within walking distance of everything. Hedrick's 4-U Motel (also serving home-cooked food) and Yokum's Vacationland (motel, cabins, camping, restaurant, and more) are both within easy driving distance.

Back on Route 33 and heading toward Harman, the road continues to wind through the steep mountains. It's about 12 miles to Harman, where you'll change onto Route 32 heading north. The road continues on to Elkins where you can join other drives (see Chapter 2 and Chapter 6).

Harman is the home of the Old Mill, a water-powered gristmill built in 1877 and located one mile north of town on Route 32. The turbines and huge millstones still function, but you must call ahead to arrange a demonstration. You'll find a variety of artifacts and many West Virginia products, including stone-ground flours, in the museum and gift shop.

Continue out of Harman on Route 32 for about six curving miles. Look for a right-hand turn onto Dry Fork Road and the Dolly Sods Wilderness Area. It's a turn into a geographical wonderland.

Just 10 miles or so down this road, which turns to gravel, sits one of the most unusual areas in a state full of outdoor wonders. The Dolly Sods Wilderness Area, taking up more than 10,000 acres within the Monongahela National Forest, is a high plateau that is more like the Canadian tundra than the West Virginia highlands. Many plant and animal species found at Dolly Sods are at their southernmost range.

The windy area is ideal for a variety of wildlife sightings, bird-watching, wildflowers, hiking, camping, and just enjoying the views that seem to last for hundreds of miles. This is

West Virginia at its wildest and an experience you won't soon forget.

Most of the high plateau is comprised of heath barrens, where the azaleas, mountain laurel, rhododendron, and blueberries seldom grow taller than chest high. Boulder-strewn areas are common on the flat plains.

The Dry Fork area is also the home of Red Creek Quarter Horse Stables. If you love horseback riding in the great outdoors, you should call in advance to check on one- and two-hour rides, half-day and full-day trips, and wilderness horseback packages.

Back on Route 32, the booming outdoor areas of Canaan Valley and Davis are just a few miles up the road. Thanks to all the outdoor opportunities, especially mountain biking, the area has become known as the Moab of the East.

Canaan Valley sits at about 3,200 feet and is surrounded by 4,000-foot-plus peaks. The mountainous terrain makes for ideal mountain-sport conditions throughout the year.

Canaan Valley State Park and Conference Center, typical of many of the state's parks, takes full advantage of Mother Nature. The list of activities is only limited by your time and sportiness: hiking, biking, golf, nature programs, camping, swimming, skiing, snowboarding, night skiing, and more in the winter. The 250-room lodge or nearby cabins make for an ideal Canaan Valley base.

The park's ski mountain is across Route 33, as is another excellent ski area, Timberline Four Seasons Resort. Timberline's wintertime claim to fame is Salamander Run, which is just under two miles long and is the longest ski trail south of New England. From spring to fall, Timberline Mountain Bike Center turns the resort into a two-wheeler's wonderland. It has many mountain rental lodging opportunities for overnighters.

The Canaan Valley area has become a popular second-home getaway. Thus, along with the state park and Timberline, there are many other support facilities established all along Route 33 for accommodations, dining, shopping, and recreation.

Just a bit past the turn for Timberline, look for the road on the right leading to White Grass Ski Touring Center. This popular cross-country skiing center, enthusiastically run by Chip Chase, features more than 30 miles of maintained trails, about 10 miles of machine-groomed trails, lessons, rentals, a pro shop, and a friendly (and warm) cafe. Whether you're a veteran or have never tried it, Timberline is well worth a visit.

Route 32 heads farther north to Davis and another major outdoor area. Thanks to Blackwater Falls State Park and the surrounding countryside, Davis has earned a reputation as a great base for outdoor adventures.

The town of Davis has an outdoor feel, with many cars loaded with mountain bikes, kayaks, canoes, and other outdoor adventure paraphernalia. The main street (Route 32) has many outdoor shops, as well as restaurants and accommodation options that welcome adventurers.

One of the biggest draws to the area is Blackwater Falls State Park, located just north of town on Route 32. Whether you stay within the park or in town, this is another West Virginia state park that shouldn't be missed.

The park is named for the falls of the Blackwater River, whose amber-colored waters plunge five stories then twist and tumble through a dramatic eight-mile gorge. The "black" water is a result of leached tannic acids from fallen hemlock and red-spruce needles. The falls are one of the most photographed sites in West Virginia.

Numerous observation points afford a panoramic view of the half-mile-wide canyon and falls. Stairways and boardwalks lead to the base of the falls for an upclose look. The quarter-mile Gentle Trail provides a quick, yet still awesome, glimpse.

Blackwater Lodge sits on the canyon's south rim, providing a sweeping view of the densely forested gorge. There are

55 guest rooms in the lodge. The lodge also has a large restaurant overlooking the canyon, which serves regional fare. There's a shop with West Virginia crafts, a sitting room, a large fireplace, and a game room.

Situated in a lovely wooded area about a mile from the lodge, you'll find 25 deluxe year-round cabins available for rent. The wooden structures feature stone fireplaces and good insulation for four-season use.

Visitors can participate in the park's year-round nature and recreation programs, including guided hikes, slide shows, movies, craft workshops, and special events. Other activities include independent hiking, horseback riding, swimming and boating in Pendleton Lake, tennis, and a small nature center. The park also features a cross-country ski center in the winter and a mountain-bike center from spring to fall.

Back in Davis, there are many other outdoor options, as well as additional places to eat and sleep. A wide variety of adventures can be pursued with the Blackwater Outdoor Center, while mountain bikers may also want to contact Blackwater Bikes or Alter Ego Sports.

For accommodations, Bright Morning and Hill House are two nice B&Bs in Davis. Both are ideal bases for biking, hiking, and much more.

You shouldn't come to Davis without experiencing a meal at Sirianni's Pizza, the place to head for fresh and tasty pizza, an eclectic atmosphere, and friendly hosts and guests. It's typical of a local business run by West Virginia natives who love their state.

If you want to take home more than memories, spend some time shopping at the Art Company of Davis and Blackwater Antiques and Art. You're sure to fall for something interesting.

The Art Company of Davis is a unique membership cooperative formed in 1990 by a small group of local artisans as a forum to exhibit their work and stimulate creativity. There are now more than 100 members who live or work in the region. The gallery is located in the old company store of the Babcock Lumber and Boom Company. Davis and Blackwater Falls State Park mark the end of this outdoor-oriented drive. Like much of West Virginia, it's a wild and wonderful way to see the state.

In the Area

Brandywine Recreation Area, George Washington National Forest (Edinburg, Virginia): (540) 984-4101

Fat Boy's Pork Palace (Brandywine): (304) 249-5591

Candlelight Inn (Franklin): (304) 358-3025

Monongahela National Forest (Elkins): (304) 636-1800

Spruce Knob (Judy Gap): (304) 257-4488

Seneca Caverns (Riverton): (304) 567-2691

Seneca Rocks Visitor Center: (304) 257-4488 or (304) 567-2827

Seneca Rocks Climbing School: (304) 567-2600 or (800) 548-0108

Seneca Rocks Mountain Guides: (304) 567-2115

Harper's Old Country Store (Seneca Rocks): (304) 567-2586

Front Porch Restaurant (Seneca Rocks): (304) 567-2555

Seneca Shadows Campground (Seneca Rocks): (800) 280-2267

Hedrick's 4-U Motel (Seneca Rocks): (304) 567-2111

Yokum's Vacationland (Seneca Rocks): (304) 567-2351

Smoke Hole Caverns (Seneca Rocks): (304) 257-4442 or (800) 828-8478 the Old Mill (Harman): (304) 227-4466

Dolly Sods Wilderness Area (Red Creek): (304) 257-4488

Red Creek Quarter Horse Stables (Dry Fork): (304) 866-4728

Canaan Valley State Park and Conference Center (Davis): (304) 866-4121, (304) 622-4121, or (800) CALL WVA

Timberline Four Seasons Resort (Davis): (304) 866-4801 or (800) 766-9464

White Grass Ski Touring Center (Canaan Valley): (304) 866-4114

Blackwater Falls State Park (Davis): (304) 259-5216 or (800) CALL WVA

Blackwater Outdoor Center (Davis): (304) 259-5117, (304) 478-4456, (800) DAVIS WV

Blackwater Bikes (Davis): (304) 259-5286

Alter Ego Sports (Davis): (304) 259-2219

Bright Morning (Davis): (304) 259-5119

Hill House (Davis): (304) 259-5883

Sirianni's Pizza (Davis): (304) 259-5454

Art Company of Davis: (304) 259-4218

Blackwater Antiques and Art (Davis): (304) 259-5625

8

The Eastern Panhandle

Getting there: From Charleston, take I-64 east to I-81 north in Virginia and continue on this all the way to Martinsburg and Route 9, which is the middle of the drive. Continue west or east on Route 9 to start the drive at either end.

Highlights: Paw Paw Tunnel, C&O Canal National Historical Park, Cacapon State Park, Coolfont Resort and Conference Center, Berkeley Springs, Martinsburg, Shepherdstown, Charles Town, Harpers Ferry. This drive is easily completed in one or two days, but it's easy to spend a week exploring the area, using Berkeley Springs, Martinsburg, Shepherdstown, or Charles Town as bases.

The eastern panhandle is definitely different from the rest of West Virginia. The proximity to Washington, D.C., makes the area a bit more cosmopolitan than many other parts of the state, but you'll still find the great outdoors, friendly people, history, and great places to stay. It's an ideal mix for a West Virginia country road drive.

This drive follows Route 9 as it runs all the way across the eastern panhandle of the state. It begins where Route 9 begins in the west, at its intersection with Route 29. Many diversions on and off Route 9 lead to a wide variety of wonderful West Virginia experiences.

The first diversion on this country road drive is actually in Maryland, before you even start heading east on Route 9. Take Route 29 just three miles north of the intersection with Route 9, head through Paw Paw and across the Potomac River to Maryland and the Paw Paw Tunnel just a quarter mile farther.

The Paw Paw Tunnel is well worth venturing out of West Virginia to see. It is, by far, the largest man-made construction on the C&O Canal and runs more than 3,000 feet through rocky Sorrell Ridge (which also has lots of pawpaw trees). The tunnel took more than 14 years to build and is now a highlight for hikers and bikers exploring the C&O Canal. If you haven't seen Maryland's C&O Canal (see *Country Roads of Maryland & Delaware*), this is a great place to do it.

The C&O Canal National Historical Park stretches beside the Potomac River from the mouth of Rock Creek in Georgetown all the way to Cumberland, Maryland (184.5 miles). It features 74 lift locks that raise the canal from near sea level to an elevation of 605 feet in Cumberland. Its towpath has become a haven for hikers, cyclists, and country road drivers escaping urban and suburban life. Other activities include canoeing, fishing, horseback riding, and many camping spots.

George Washington originally thought of a waterway connecting the Chesapeake Bay with the Ohio Valley. By 1802, canals were cut to get around the five falls of the Potomac River, but expansion did not occur until the mid-1800s. By the time the C&O Canal reached Cumberland in 1850, it had already been shown that trains were more efficient. It was badly damaged by a flood in 1889 and again in 1924, as commercial traffic came to a halt.

The canal became a national monument in 1961 and was named a national historical park in 1971. It winds through the Piedmont on the Allegheny plateau, right past the Great Falls of the Potomac and through the ridge and valley section of the Appalachian Mountains.

Back in West Virginia, you can spend the night at the Paw Paw Patch Bed & Breakfast before starting down Route 9. At the start of the drive south of Paw Paw, you immediately head into Morgan County. The winding road parallels the twisting Cacapon River as it makes its way through the pretty county.

The river's namesake park, Cacapon State Park, runs alongside Route 9 and its entrance is on the right about 10 miles into the drive. It's well worth a diversion for a few hours or a few days. Cacapon State Park stretches from the Virginia border to within five miles of the Potomac River and West Virginia's northern border with Maryland. The long and narrow 6,000-acre retreat offers a wide range of recreational activities.

Cacapon Mountain, at 2,300 feet, is the dominant feature within the park, following its length north and south. Hiking and bridle trails, as well as a road, climb 1,400 feet to the summit. Spur trails along the ridge bring hikers to large rock outcrops of resistant sandstone and offer spectacular views of the valley below.

Awaiting visitors in the secluded woodlands are 13 standard, 11 deluxe, and 6 economy log cabins, with wood-paneled walls, stone fireplaces, and kitchens. The cabins are generally open from mid-April through the end of October.

Cacapon Lodge sits in the broad valley on the east side of the mountain. The 50-room facility also features a popular lounge, fireplace, restaurant, and crafts shop.

The Old Inn, situated near the lodge, was originally built in the 1930s by the Civilian Conservation Corps and offers 11 rooms in an historic and rustic atmosphere. Low ceilings, stone chimneys, and wrought-iron hardware add to the effect.

The inn also features a large dining room and kitchen. The North Fork of Indian Run flows within footsteps of the inn's stone veranda.

Recreational activities at Cacapon are quite diverse. There's hiking and horseback riding on 27 miles of trails, running past laurel, pine, and mixed hardwood forests to scenic vistas atop Cacapon Mountain. Guests can swim, fish, and boat at spring- and stream-fed Cacapon Lake. Various games, including tennis and volleyball, are available for a small fee. Guests can also participate in the park's nature and recreation programs, including guided hikes, slide shows, craft workshops, and movies. With enough snow, cross-country skiers can use the golf course, as long as they stay off the greens and tees.

The golf course, designed by Robert Trent Jones, has been rated as one of the best-designed courses in the country. The rolling terrain at the foot of the mountain is ideal for golf, with highlights including more than 70 sandtraps and a unique 100-yard-wide green that is shared by the fourth and eighth holes.

About seven miles after the park, look for the pulloff for Prospect Peak on the left. This stunning spot, once covered by *National Geographic*, features great views of the river below.

Once you pull yourself away from Prospect Peak, Route 9 leads to many more pleasures. Just two miles after leaving the peak and just before getting to Berkeley Springs, look for the sign on the right to Coolfont Resort and Conference Center.

Situated on 1,200 acres in a hidden valley between Cacapon Mountain and Warm Springs Ridge, family-owned Coolfont is West Virginia recreation and relaxation at its finest. You'll find a friendly and relaxed environment, whether you're there for a special weekend dinner or a week.

When you first see the resort, you see mountain vistas, two sparkling spring-fed lakes, and the beautiful Treetop

House Restaurant, a famous restaurant high in the trees. Only later do you realize that hidden in the unspoiled landscape are a variety of accommodation, relaxation, and recreational facilities, including a lodge, chalets, vacation homes, and a conference center.

There's a wide range of accommodations, including nice lodge rooms and beautiful two-bedroom and two-bath chalets in the woods, with whirlpool tubs, woodburning fire stoves, and outdoor decks. Coolfont recreation possibilities include indoor swimming, tennis, whirlpool tubs, a fitness center, concerts, hiking, fishing, spa pampering, massages, spa retreats, boating, stop-smoking programs, and some of the state's finest dining opportunities. If you're in the eastern panhandle, you'll quickly warm to a Coolfont stay.

Berkeley Springs is just down the hill on Route 9. In a region where George Washington seems to have slept, eaten, or visited everywhere, this town can claim that George Washington bathed there. Washington recognized the restorative powers of the springs, as did Indians before him and as do today's visitors.

Originally established as the town of Bath in 1776, Berkeley Springs became one of America's most popular spa destinations in the eighteenth century. In this century, it is returning to its former fame.

The curing waters are drawing many visitors. The springs discharge the 74.3-degree water and the faithful drink it, sit in it, and much more. Combine that with great places to stay, eat, and visit, and you have a unique place to spend several days.

Berkeley Springs State Park is at the center of it all, right in the middle of town. This unique seven-acre park features an 1815 Roman bathhouse, with private 750-gallon bathing pools, a fascinating museum, a popular public tap, the stone tub used by Washington, and the main bathhouse, where a variety of "treatment" packages are offered at remarkably reasonable prices.

A main bathhouse package is something you'll never forget. The old state-run facility offers a variety of baths, steams, showers, and massages. You'll leave relaxed and intrigued by the unusual experience. It's a refreshing contrast to some of the luxurious spa resorts of today.

The area around the state park is packed with things to see and do. If you're not staying at Coolfont, you should definitely consider the Country Inn (or a stay at both).

Since 1932, the Country Inn has afforded rest and relaxation to countless visitors who have discovered Berkeley Springs and this resort. The inn, which is all brick and of colonial design, is well-known for comfortable accommodations, an inviting colonial dining room, the Wayfarer's Lounge, and the porches and lawns that adjoin the village green and the state park.

The Renaissance Spa is another relaxing reminder of why you're in Berkeley Springs and at the Country Inn. This full-service spa features private whirlpool baths, massage, facials, makeup application, manicures, pedicures, hairstyling, and a boutique. A large number of spa and other packages, which include accommodations, are available at the Country Inn.

The rest of Berkeley Springs is just as interesting. Travel Berkeley Springs, at 304 Fairfax Street, can provide walking-tour maps and other information about accommodations, dining, shopping, antiquing, and many special events (the Winter Festival of the Waters from January to March, and April's Unique WV: Wine, Food, and Folk Arts Festival are both popular).

One of the highlights in town is Berkeley Castle, an 1885 sandstone replica of Berkeley Castle in England. The town's dinner theater is a special treat on weekend nights.

Back in town, you can shop 'til you drop and then enjoy a rejuvenating massage. As you would expect, many of the excellent shops revolve around health and fitness. Two of the best are the Bath House and Homeopathy Works, both on

Fairfax Street. The Bath House is a complete
health center that also offers books, gifts, massages, a catalog, and much more.

Homeopathy Works features a retail
outlet, classes, and a homeopathy museum.
Homeopathy is a comprehensive approach to
medical treatment that was developed by German
physician Samuel Hahnemann more than 200 years ago. Vir-
tually all of the 1,200 or so nontoxic remedies are available
without prescription and are made from botanical, animal,
mineral, and chemical substances. The museum displays feature more than 200 years of homeopathic history, including
handcrafted oak cabinets housing hundreds of bottles of
remedies in tinctures and tablets.

Antique shopping is also another popular Berkeley Springs
activity. The Berkeley Springs Antique Mall offers a wide variety of choices from a number of vendors.

If all this healthy activity (or relaxation) makes you hungry, you have several fun choices right in town. For casual dining with lots of locals, try Tari's: A Premier Cafe & Inn, a fun
place personally run by Tari. For a literally religious dining
experience, head to Maria's Garden & Inn, where owner Peg
Perry features great food and a huge collection of religious
objects dedicated to the Virgin Mary. Regional cooking can be
found at the Appalachian Restaurant.

If you can't stay at Coolfont or the Country Inn, or want
a small B&B experience instead, Berkeley Springs has several
perfect possibilities. The Glens offers huge rooms on its 14
acres. The Highlawn Inn offers a hilltop view amidst Victorian elegance. Aaron's Acre features a charming restored farmhouse and five guest rooms reminiscent of a bygone era. Tari's
and Maria's Garden & Inn also have nice rooms for rent.

As you leave Berkeley Springs completely relaxed, you'll
need your strength for the wonderful shopping and sightseeing possibilities in Martinsburg. The half-hour drive from

Berkeley Springs passes by the entrance to the Woods and through the town of Hedgesville, both of which offer additional accommodation options.

The Woods is a premier golf resort that has become a popular retirement and second-home haven. But the Woods also offers deluxe lodging, dining, and golf to visitors passing through. If you love golf, it's a great place to stop.

Near the small town of Hedgesville, you'll find the big B&B—the Farmhouse on Tomahawk Run. Hugh and Judy Erskine welcome guests in their special country home, with large rooms and balconies, private baths, whirlpool, three-course candlelight breakfasts, 280 acres of woods and meadows, and a self-contained carriage house apartment. The Farmhouse is nestled in a quiet valley next to the historic tomahawk-shaped spring for which the area was named. It was built by Judy's great grandfather during the Civil War on land occupied by her ancestors since the 1740s.

Martinsburg is an interesting stop for many reasons. It's known for shopping (and for good reason), but this quaint town also has a wide array of historic and modern attractions.

Martinsburg was laid out in 1773 by Gen. Adam Stephen and was incorporated in 1778. Thus, it has a wealth of architecturally historic buildings.

In 1843, the B&O Railroad brought new growth and prosperity to the town. At the time, large warehouses and hotels were erected, as well as new industrial complexes. Martinsburg's location and railroad brought it much attention during the Civil War, as the city suffered great physical and emotional scarring.

In the late 1940s, Martinsburg began attracting many new businesses, which continues today with the growth of high-tech industry and governmental agencies. The railroad still flourishes with freight, but it also provides daily commuter rail service to the Washington, D.C., metropolitan area.

The Martinsburg-Berkeley County Convention & Visitors Bureau, at 208 South Queen Street, can provide an historic walking-tour map, as well as information about shopping, accommodations, and dining. A walking tour really reveals the wealth of architecture and history in this small city.

Along with a wide variety of interesting houses in the large national historic district, several special places include the Belle Boyd House (the former home of a Confederate spy and now the Berkeley County and Civil War Museums), the General Adam Stephen House (the 1789 limestone home of a surgeon and American Revolution officer), the Triple Brick House (an 1874 apartment house), and the Boarman Arts Center (an active arts gallery).

There is also historic shopping in Martinsburg, which draws thousands of visitors. Unlike many outlet shopping centers, the Blue Ridge Outlet Center is clean, attractive, well run, and full of bargains.

Historic turn-of-the-century woolen mills have been transformed into an authentic manufacturers' outlet, featuring brands you'd never dream of finding at such low prices. You can save on products from companies like American Eagle, Anne Klein, Arrow, Britches, Champion, Corning/Revere Ware, Dansk, Aigner, J. Crew, Johnston & Murphy Footwear, L'eggs/Hanes/Bali, London Fog, Ralph Lauren, Van Heusen, fine glassmakers from West Virginia, and much more.

Other shopping stops include Panhandle Pottery and Designs, Stephen Street Emporium, Wright's Stained Glass & Custom Art, and many other stores that seem to fill Martinsburg's busy streets. Many shoppers will want to make Martinsburg their eastern panhandle base. Quaint in-city accommodation options include the Boydville Inn Bed and Breakfast, the Pulpit & Palette Inn, and the Aspen Hall Inn.

For shopping energy, you need to eat. The American Deli in the Blue Ridge Outlet Center is a popular spot, as are the Market House Grill and Ramon's in town.

Continue out of Martinsburg for about six miles until

Route 480, where a left-hand turn will take you toward another Route 9 diversion that deserves a few hours or several days. The Route 480 intersection is in Kearneysville, a small town with a number of craftspeople working out of their homes (just look for signs). Five miles up Route 480, historic Shepherdstown and the Bavarian Inn and Lodge await the arrival of many country road drivers.

Shepherdstown and its surroundings hold fascination for any visitor seeking to savor a small town and big history. The oldest town in what is now West Virginia started out as Mecklenburg in 1762, but was renamed Shepherd's Town in 1798 in honor of its founder, Thomas Shepherd. It became Shepherdstown in 1867, when it was granted a charter by the new state of West Virginia.

Military buffs know the town was the jumping-off point for the legendary Bee Line March, in which the first large contingent of southern volunteers hiked overland in record time to help George Washington's fledgling Continental army.

The Civil War never quite came to town, but the battle of Antietam was fought less than five miles away across the Potomac. After the battle, Shepherdstown became an impromptu hospital for Robert E. Lee's retreating Confederate army.

The town's claim to be the birthplace of the steamboat is based on the achievements of James Rumsey, who built and successfully demonstrated a working steamboat on the Potomac River at Shepherdstown 20 years before Robert Fulton's *Claremont* first steamed up the Hudson River. In 1987, in time for the bicentennial of his achievement, volunteers aiding the Rumseian Society built a replica of Rumsey's boat, which is now on display at the Historic Shepherdstown Museum. A James Rumsey Monument overlooks the Potomac just outside of town.

Shepherd College plays a big role in the life of this pretty town. It was founded in 1871 and its pretty campus is enjoyable for strolling. The college has given cultural vibrancy to Shepherdstown, drawing many artists to the area.

This small college town is easy to explore on foot. There are many historic eighteenth- and nineteenth-century commercial and residential buildings. Shopping, dining, lodging, and cultural events all reveal Shepherdstown's cosmopolitan nature. There's even a Sunday-morning market, where you'll find fresh bread, vegetables, flowers, and friendly locals. The Shepherdstown Visitor Information Center can provide a walking-tour map, as well as accommodation, dining, and shopping options.

The old Entler Hotel houses the Historic Shepherdstown Museum. The hotel opened in 1786 and was run by the Entler family until 1912, when it was used for a variety of things. In its current use as a museum it features a wide variety of antiques, artifacts, photos, and more pertaining to the town's history.

Across the street, you'll find the Yellow Brick Bank Restaurant, a fancy beaux arts building you can't miss. The food is as creative as the architecture. Other dining possibilities in town include the Old Pharmacy Cafe & Soda Fountain and Town Run Deli.

Shopping is also a big tourist activity in town. Among many unique shops, you may want to try Earthwalk, Herb Lady (also in Harpers Ferry), Shepherdstown Book Shop, and Ye Olde Sweet Shoppe Bakery for that sweet tooth.

Just outside town, on Washington Street at Toll House Turn, O'Hurley's General Store is an unusual shopping attraction. This incredible country store re-creation, owned by friendly Jay Hurley, features a seemingly infinite number of turn-of-the-century goods, as well as more current items. It's well worth several hours of searching to find just the right thing.

As can be expected, the town also has many B&Bs and inns that cater to visitors. Two top choices are the Thomas Shepherd Inn and Gay Shepherd Henderson's Bellevue Bed & Breakfast. Just outside town, Ann Small's Stonebrake Cottage Guest House offers a Victorian retreat.

The Thomas Shepherd Inn is typical of Shepherdstown hospitality. Margaret Perry and Connie Imbach welcome visitors to this inn, situated on the corner of German and Duke Streets, with six pleasant guest rooms, private baths, a living room, two formal dining rooms, a library, a popular porch, afternoon tea, home-cooked breakfast, and even a romantic dinner, if arranged in advance.

With all its great sightseeing, shopping, dining, and accommodations, Shepherdstown features one more thing that draws visitors from throughout the region: the Bavarian Inn and Lodge, one of West Virginia's most popular destinations.

The award-winning Bavarian Inn and Lodge is owned and hosted by a native Bavarian from Munich, Erwin Asam, and his British wife, Carol, as well as their sons, Christian and David. From the meals to the rooms to the people, you'll find gracious old-world hospitality.

Set on 11 acres of grassy lawns overlooking the Potomac River, the Greystone Mansion houses the Bavarian Inn's famous restaurant. The bright dining rooms are decorated with antiques and deer-horn chandeliers. The cuisine features German and American specialties for breakfast, lunch, and dinner. The menu changes seasonally, with the possibilities including spring lamb, veal specialties, fresh seafood, and hearty game dishes like roast pheasant, venison, and wild boar. The tasty baked breads and desserts are prepared daily. Below the dining room, the cozy Rathskeller offers casual dining, a bar, and entertainment on weekends.

The grounds feature four chalets, in Bavarian alpine motif, that house 72 elegantly furnished guest rooms. With balconies that overlook the Potomac River, most rooms have fireplaces, queen-size canopied four-poster beds, and sitting areas with sleep sofas.

The inn also offers an outdoor pool with a sun deck overlooking the Potomac, a modern exercise room, bicycle rentals, and a lit tennis court. Even if you never step foot in Shepherdstown, the Bavarian Inn and Lodge is a destination in itself.

Head back to Route 9 by way of Route 480 and take the left at Kearneysville for the seven-mile drive into Charles Town. The last three miles involve speeding along a four-lane highway, which belies the quiet historic charm of Charles Town, just ahead.

Founded in 1786 by an act of the Virginia legislature, on land donated by George Washington's youngest brother, Charles, this town has a long and interesting history. George fell in love with the area as an 18-year-old surveyor, investing his first earnings in 550 acres and later enlarging it to 2,300 acres. Charles inherited the land and a love for it from George. He eventually laid out the town, much as it is today, including the donation of four corner lots for use as government buildings.

Today, you can see the historic legacy of the Washington family and much more. The raid on Harpers Ferry by abolitionist John Brown brought Charles Town into the limelight in 1859, while Brown was held prisoner in the Charles Town jail (now a post office), tried, convicted, and executed by hanging.

During the Civil War, Charles Town was ravaged by two major battles, as well as by Gen. Philip Sheridan during the opening of his Shenandoah Valley campaign. Thankfully, many buildings were left standing.

Charles Town Main Street has published an informative walking-tour brochure that is available at many establishments, as well as at the Jefferson County Convention & Visitors Bureau on Route 340. You can see most of the structures in the 11-block area in a few hours, including Happy Retreat, Charles Washington's home.

Historical points of interest include the courthouse, where John Brown was tried; the post office, where he was held prisoner; and the Old Opera House, which now features performing arts. The Zion Episcopal Church nearby surely has the greatest number of Washington family descendents (more than 80) on its grounds, including 20 family members who were born at Mount Vernon.

In addition to the architectural and historical wonders, you may want to stop by the Jefferson County Museum, housed in the library at 200 East Washington Street. Thousands of artifacts include papers relating to the Washington family, the cot on which the wounded John Brown lay during his trial, the wagon in which Brown rode to his execution, and much more.

Charles Town is a great base for exploring the eastern panhandle. If you plan to spend the night, contact one of the many B&Bs and inns in or around town: Carriage Inn Bed & Breakfast, Cottonwood Inn, Hillbrook Inn (a country house hotel), and the Washington House Inn Bed & Breakfast.

Most of the accommodation options are located in historic houses, with many interesting stories from the past. For instance, hosts Bob and Virginia Kaetzel at the Carriage Inn will tell you that the house hosted Generals U. S. Grant and Philip Sheridan in the east parlor in 1864, when they discussed Civil War strategy in the Shenandoah Valley. Over at the Washington House, Mel and Nina Vogel will explain how their Victorian house was built at the turn of the century by descendents of George Washington's brothers, John Augustine and Samuel.

The dining scene in Charles Town is equally historic. The Charles Washington Inn dates from the eighteenth century, and the old-fashioned food is fresh and tasty. The restaurant is nestled between two sycamore trees in a 1788 house built by Dr. Edward Tiffin on land bought from Charles Washington.

To pay for your accommodations and meals, why not test Lady Luck at the Charles Town Turf Club for a day or night of thoroughbred racing? This pretty old racetrack features the sport of kings year-round. You might even make some gas money for more country road driving.

Route 340 heads out of Charles Town to Harpers Ferry, and though the busy road isn't particularly interesting, the end result of this drive is typically historic.

About halfway along the five-mile drive to Harpers Ferry, look for the Fruit & Veggie Wagon on the left-hand side of the road, at the intersection of Route 340 and Country Club Road. This store offers lots of local fruits and vegetables, cider, jams, jellies, and flowers.

Also about halfway to Harpers Ferry, look for Blue Ridge Outfitters, one of several outdoor-oriented companies taking advantage of the scenic Shenandoah and Potomac Rivers. Since 1972, Blue Ridge Outfitters has offered rafting trips on the two beautiful rivers that meet at Harpers Ferry. Its most popular trip is on the Shenandoah's final section, before it merges with the mighty Potomac. Expert guides lead the rafts and rafters through White Horse Rapids, down the famed Shenandoah Staircase, and even over Bull Falls. You'll float right by historic Harpers Ferry and enjoy lunch before or after the three- to five-hour trip.

Blue Ridge Outfitters also offers Potomac River trips below Great Falls, from its Potomac outpost near Washington, D.C., as well as fishing, canoeing, tubing, camping, and leadership and team development programs. Blue Ridge Outfitters is the complete eastern panhandle outdoor outfitter.

The Jefferson County Convention & Visitors Bureau sits directly across from the left-hand turn for Harpers Ferry

National Historic Park. This helpful office has a variety of brochures for the area. It's best to follow the signs to the official park entrance and parking for Harpers Ferry National Historic Park, rather than trying to find a rare parking space in Harpers Ferry proper. Helpful visitor center personnel can answer questions, provide maps, and get you on the frequent shuttle into town, where you'll be deposited into another world. Situated at the confluence of the Shenandoah and Potomac Rivers in the shadow of the Blue Ridge Mountains, Harpers Ferry became an important industrialized transportation hub and arms-producing town in the eighteenth and nineteenth centuries.

The town gained national attention on the night of October 16, 1859, with John Brown's infamous raid. Brown was a staunch abolitionist who devised a plan to liberate slaves through violence, setting up a stronghold in the mountains of Maryland and Virginia. His operation started with an insurrection in Harpers Ferry, with Brown choosing the town because of its location near the Mason-Dixon Line, easy access to the mountains for guerilla warfare, and large stock of arms. Brown and his 21-man army seized the armory and other strategic points before the townspeople could react.

The militia of Harpers Ferry finally cornered Brown and his men in the armory fire engine and guard house (now called John Brown's Fort). They were captured on the morning of the 18th, by a contingent of marines led by Col. Robert E. Lee and Lt. J. E. B. Stuart.

John Brown was tried for murder, treason, and conspiring with slaves to create insurrection. He was found guilty and hanged in Charles Town on December 2, 1859.

On that day, Brown wrote a prophetic note to the nation: "I, John Brown, am now quite certain that the crimes of this guilty land will never be purged away but with blood. I had, as I now think, vainly flattered myself that without very much bloodshed it might be done." The Civil War started a short 16 months later on April 12, 1861, at Fort Sumter in Charleston, South Carolina.

Harpers Ferry was devastated during the Civil War. Because of its strategic location, the town was occupied by both sides and suffered through many major battles. The Union Army burned the armory and arsenal buildings in 1861 to keep them from being captured by Confederate troops.

Many people left the war-ravaged town, which went through additional damage from a series of devastating floods in the late 1800s. It fell into decay before serious restoration work in the 1960s by the government saved the town for all to visit.

Today, the Harpers Ferry National Historic Park is a national treasure. The shuttle bus deposits visitors in the middle of restored historic buildings, exhibits, shops, and restaurants. The park map is perfect for an extensive walking tour, which starts in the information center housed in the old Stagecoach Inn, run by Maj. James Stephenson from 1826–34. It's now a great place for drinking in plenty of historical information.

Along Shenandoah Street, many buildings evoke the boom days of Harpers Ferry. The re-created Provost Office shows the wartime office of the Union provost guard. The Dry Goods Store, built in 1812, depicts a typical dry goods store of the mid-1800s. Next door, the Master Armorer's House serves as a fascinating museum concerning the history of gunmaking.

Farther down Shenandoah Street, the John Brown Museum houses a theater and museum relating the events of John Brown's historic raid. Across the street, John Brown's Fort (the old fire engine house) has been restored. Behind the fort, there's a great view of Maryland and Virginia across the rivers.

St. Peter's Catholic Church looms over the landscape of Harpers Ferry. Hearty walkers can make their way up the stone steps (cut into natural rock in the 1800s) to the pretty

1830s church. Even farther up sits Jefferson Rock, offering a view Thomas Jefferson said was "worth a voyage across the Atlantic."

Back in town, High Street and Potomac Street offer more museums, shops, and restaurants. The Civil War Museum and the Black History Exhibit are particularly interesting.

Once you see Harpers Ferry, you're sure to want to stay more than a day. The quaint town features many appropriate accommodation options: Between the Rivers, Filmore Street B&B, Harpers Ferry Guest House, Lee Stonewall Inn, and the Ranson-Armory House. They are all individually owned and operated and are located in the heart of the historic district.

For historic meals, the Anvil Restaurant is one of many popular choices in town or just up the hill. The Hilltop House Hotel, Restaurant, & Conference Center offers excellent meals and views (as well as a scenic place to stay).

Harpers Ferry is also conveniently near the C&O Canal National Historical Park and the Appalachian Trail. The Appalachian National Scenic Trail is one of the world's greatest hiking trails. The famed Appalachian Trail is a 2,144-mile

Historic Harpers Ferry

hiking path along the ridge of the Appalachian Mountains, stretching from Georgia to Maine. It runs through 14 states to the finish at Katahdin, Maine.

The first section of the Appalachian Trail was constructed in New Jersey in 1922. The Appalachian Mountain Club got involved, as did many individuals. With the help of the Civilian Conservation Corps, many hiking clubs, and thousands of other volunteers, all sections of the Appalachian Trail were finally relocated, opened, and marked for hikers and outdoor lovers in 1951.

In 1968, the National Trails Systems Act made the Appalachian Trail a linear national park and authorized funds to surround the entire route with public lands. The Appalachian Trail is now maintained by a variety of active local clubs and government agencies. The Appalachian Trail Conference, based in Harpers Ferry, is in constant need of volunteers all along the Appalachian Trail.

The Appalachian Trail serves as a great retreat from eastern urban life—more than two-thirds of the nation's population lives within 550 miles of it. Due to the Appalachian Trail headquarters location, Harpers Ferry is a mecca for hikers. It's a great way to end an exploration of West Virginia's eastern panhandle.

In the Area

Paw Paw Tunnel, C&O Canal (Paw Paw): (301) 739-4200

C&O Canal National Historical Park (Great Falls, Maryland): (301) 739-4200

Paw Paw Patch Bed & Breakfast: (304) 947-7496

Cacapon State Park (Berkeley Springs): (304) 258-1022 or (800) CALL WVA

Coolfont Resort and Conference Center (Berkeley Springs): (304) 258-4500 or (800) 888-8768

Berkeley Springs State Park: (304) 258-2711 or (800) CALL WVA

Country Inn (Berkeley Springs): (304) 258-2210 or (800) 822-6630

Travel Berkeley Springs: (304) 258-9147 or (800) 447-8797

the Bath House (Berkeley Springs): (304) 258-9071 or (800) 431-4698

Homeopathy Works (Berkeley Springs): (304) 258-2541

Berkeley Springs Antique Mall: (304) 258-5676

Tari's: A Premier Cafe & Inn (Berkeley Springs): (304) 258-1196

Maria's Garden & Inn (Berkeley Springs): (304) 258-2021

the Appalachian Restaurant (Berkeley Springs): (304) 258-3110

the Glens (Berkeley Springs): (304) 258-GLENS

Highlawn Inn (Berkeley Springs): (304) 258-5700

Aaron's Acre (Berkeley Springs): (304) 258-4079

the Woods (Hedgesville): (304) 754-7977 or (800) 248-2222

the Farmhouse on Tomahawk Run (Hedgesville): (304) 754-7350

Martinsburg-Berkeley County Convention & Visitors Bureau: (304) 264-8801 or (800) 498-2386

Blue Ridge Outlet Center (Martinsburg): (304) 254-4566 or (800) 445-3993

Panhandle Pottery and Designs (Martinsburg): (304) 264-0478

Stephen Street Emporium (Martinsburg): (304) 264-9130 or (800) 249-9130

Wright's Stained Glass & Custom Art (Martinsburg): (304) 263-2502

Boydville Inn Bed and Breakfast (Martinsburg): (304) 263-1448

Pulpit & Palette Inn (Martinsburg): (304) 263-7012

Aspen Hall Inn (Martinsburg): (304) 263-4385

American Deli (Martinsburg): (304) 263-4656

Market House Grill (Martinsburg): (304) 263-7615

Ramon's (Martinsburg): (304) 263-2989

Historic Shepherdstown Museum: (304) 876-0910

Shepherdstown Visitor Information Center: (304) 876-3325

Yellow Brick Bank Restaurant (Shepherdstown): (304) 876-2208

Old Pharmacy Cafe & Soda Fountain (Shepherdstown): (304) 876-2085

Town Run Deli (Shepherdstown): (304) 876-3200

Earthwalk (Shepherdstown): (304) 876-3969

Herb Lady (Shepherdstown): (304) 876-9436

Shepherdstown Book Shop: (304) 876-9491

Ye Olde Sweet Shoppe Bakery (Shepherdstown): (304) 876-2432 or (800) 9 BAKERY

O'Hurley's General Store (Shepherdstown): (304) 876-6907

Thomas Shepherd Inn (Shepherdstown): (304) 876-3715

Bellevue Bed & Breakfast (Shepherdstown): (304) 876-0889

Stonebrake Cottage Guest House (Shepherdstown): (304) 876-6607

Charles Town Main Street: (304) 535-2627

Old Opera House (Charles Town): (304) 725-4420

Carriage Inn Bed & Breakfast (Charles Town): (304) 728-8003

Cottonwood Inn (Charles Town): (304) 725-3371

Hillbrook Inn (Charles Town): (304) 725-4223

Washington House Inn Bed & Breakfast (Charles Town): (304) 725-7923

Charles Washington Inn (Charles Town): (304) 725-4020

Charles Town Turf Club: (304) 725-7001

Fruit & Veggie Wagon (Charles Town): (304) 725-7110

Blue Ridge Outfitters (Charles Town): (304) 725-3444

Jefferson County Convention & Visitors Bureau (Harpers Ferry): (304) 535-2627 or (800) 848-8687

Harpers Ferry National Historic Park: (304) 535-6223

Between the Rivers (Harpers Ferry): (304) 535-2768

Filmore Street B&B (Harpers Ferry): (304) 535-2619

Harpers Ferry Guest House: (304) 535-6955

Lee Stonewall Inn (Harpers Ferry): (304) 535-2532

Ranson-Armory House (Harpers Ferry): (304) 535-2142

the Anvil Restaurant (Harpers Ferry): (304) 535-2582

Hilltop House Hotel, Restaurant, & Conference Center (Harpers Ferry): (304) 535-2132 or (800) 338-8319

Appalachian Trail Conference (Harpers Ferry): (304) 535-6331

Index